Look Out Satan

~

God's At Work!

A Memoir
By: Bill Davis

Copyright @ 2022

Coastal Winds Publishing House

Coastal Winds Publishing House
3167 63rd Street, Port Arthur, Texas 77640
Publisher: Pamela Licatino

Copyright @ 2022 by Bill Davis

All rights reserved. No part of this book shall be reproduced, stored in a retrieval system, or transmitted by any means, electronic, mechanical, photocopied, recorded, or otherwise, without explicit written permission by author and/or publisher. No liability is assumed for any damages resulting from the contents or use of information contained within.

For information, contact: Coastal Winds Publishing House
Email: coastalwindspublishing@live.com

ISBN: 979-8-218-07848-5
Library of Congress Control Number: 2022946861

Editor: Cheryl Davis, Groves, Texas

Cover Design and layout: Pamela Joy Licatino, Illustrator

Printing and Distribution: Lightning Source/Ingram

Book Reviews

Look Out Satan ~ God's At Work! is an amazing Christian book! It tells of different struggles Sgt. Davis endured and how God guided him through them all! This book is definitely one I will read time and time again, especially when I need an extra push in life! I 10/10 recommend reading this book. You won't regret it!
        Ellie Mae
        New York

WOW! I admire you for doing this kind of work, God's work, for such a long time! I am a registered nurse and I know what burnout is. This is definitely the kind of work that could burn you out. But, you stuck with it! I loved how you were so descriptive in everything – BeBe and the pretty nurse with the catheter. It's like we (the reader) are right there with you - solving cases, Crime Stoppers, almost a Texas Ranger, almost a judge! You are continuing to do God's work!
        Wanda Travis, R.N.
        Groves, TX

Bill immediately grabs your attention with his real life accounts and transported me back in time with a flood of emotions of my own life experiences. As adoptive parents of children that were rescued from abuse and abusive situations, Bill's real life stories are heart-wrenching and attention-grabbing. His attention to detail in his detective work and the love of freeing children from abusive situations is inspiring and full of hope.
        Pastors Mike and Tina Halliburton
        New Covenant Church
        Port Arthur, TX

Look Out Satan ~ God's At Work!
The memoir is enjoyable reading - great stories and experiences. And, I enjoyed it particularly because Bill and Cheryl are friends of mine. Bill and my late husband, Craig, were very good friends, so it was a joy and pleasure to read his story. Congratulations Bill, on another great book!

                                  Brenda Bruno
                                  Lumberton, TX

Throughout our personal friendship, I have heard most of these stories. But, I never knew a lot of the details you have explained in this book. To me, it was RIVETING!!!!!

Thank you for your efforts.

                                  Rick Lute
                                  Bridge City, TX

Acknowledgment

My acknowledgment is to my Lord and Savior, Jesus Christ. Without Him, I am nothing. As major incidents occurred throughout my life, I would ask "Why?" In His time, He would always provide the answer, which was always above and beyond what I thought was best for me. The words for this book came from Him. I pray that He is honored and glorified by this undertaking.

Should someone read this book who does not know my Lord as their personal Savior, my prayer is for them to come to know Him and realize how wonderful it is to be royalty, a child of the Most High God – a child of the King of Kings and Lord of Lords!

If your goal in reading this book is to only grasp my physical injuries, then you missed the whole point. **My thought is – don't read it!**

Many of our military men and women and first responders, our true heroes, have experienced physical injuries far greater than mine. However, I believe this book delivers a Spiritual message that will touch everyone's heart.

We are all made in the image of God. He put us on this earth to do a job – to accept His Son, Jesus, as our Lord and Savior, work every day to be closer to Him, and do a job to honor Him. I believe God allows negative things to happen to us to test our love and reliance on Him. The programs I present are not mine, but HIS. I believe HE appointed me to present them to save HIS children from abuse and neglect.

Satan tried to stop me – but **LOST!**

Psalms 23

(The Holy Bible – New King James Version)

The Lord is my shepherd, I shall not want.
He makes me lie down in green pastures;
He leads me beside the still waters.
He restores my soul;
He leads me in the paths of righteousness for His name's sake.
Yea, though I walk through the valley of the shadow of death,
I will fear no evil, for You are with me;
Your rod and Your staff, they comfort me.
You prepare a table before me in the presence of my enemies;
You anoint my head with oil; My cup runs over.
Surely goodness and mercy shall follow me
all the days of my life,
And I will dwell in the house of the Lord forever.

Table of Contents

Prologue	....	14
Chapter One	January 7, 1984..	16
Chapter Two	Hospitals, Doctors, & Nurses...................	36
Chapter Three	Aftercare...	49
Chapter Four	Dusty...	57
Chapter Five	Back to Work..	69
Chapter Six	God's Preparations...................................	78
Chapter Seven	A Program Is Born...................................	105
Chapter Eight	Just Getting Started..................................	112
Chapter Nine	Faith vs. Fear...	123
Chapter Ten	True Crime Books....................................	138
Chapter Eleven	More Programs...	160
Chapter Twelve	God Really Does Work In Mysterious Ways!...	180
Epilogue	So... What <u>Really</u> Happened January 7, 1984?.......................................	197
Thoughtful Poems	....	205
History	....	211
True Crime Books	....	219
Presentations	....	225
Photos	65-68; 76-77; 102-104; 111; 120-122; 136-137; 159; 176-178; 194-196; 233-243	
A Blessing	....	245

Dear Reader,

It is with humble gratitude that I thank you for reading my latest book, **Look Out Satan ~ God's At Work!**

All of the facts are correct. However, several of the people named in the book are deceased or have moved, or it would be quite difficult to obtain written permission to use their names in the script. Therefore, some of the names have been changed for legal reasons.

                                          Bill Davis

Prologue

"Take heed that you do not despise one of these little ones, for I say to you that in heaven their angels always see the face of My Father who is in heaven." Matthew 18:10 - NKJV

The elementary school guest just finished his presentation on child safety. He knelt to talk to the kindergarten students as the first and second graders walked single file back to their classrooms from the cafetorium. His police uniform was neatly pressed, his black boots, gun belt, holster and other leather items were all polished. The children touched his shiny badge. They asked to see his gun. He told them it was not a toy and not to be played with. They could look at in it the holster. The big gun remained there. Then he let them touch his right wrist. The children remembered the policeman telling them the story of how he was shot by a man with a shotgun. They touched the nub where his right thumb used to be. They touched the scar on his inner forearm. And then he let them touch one of the #6 shotgun pellets that were still in his body. He felt for a moment and then he found it, just below his ribs in his upper abdomen. Each of them could feel the little round, hard shotgun BB under his skin through his t-shirt. Some of them hollered "Ugh." Some of them said, "Wow!" Their teacher smiled at their fascination. She was glad her principal and counselor scheduled this man who spoke so easily on the level of her children and communicated with them well. She even told him that the children would keep him there all day telling stories and asking questions, if she would let them. She gently told them it was time to go. These little ones would never forget their new friend, 'Officer Bill.'

Presenting a safety program to these little children never got old, even though Sgt. Bill Davis had been presenting his *'Child Safety: First & Forever with Officer Bill'* program at hundreds of elementary schools to thousands of students, since he created the program in 1985. His goal was to save one of them, and then to save one more.

It wasn't always easy showing his injured hand and forearm to people. Many times, in the beginning shortly after the accident, he got mad. At times he even yelled at God and demanded an answer, "Why me?" God would reveal Himself and His reasons to this veteran police officer in due time. It would take time. It would take years. Slowly, but surely, God would reveal His reason. Bill had to learn to listen to that quiet, small voice.

"Oh, the depth of the riches and wisdom and knowledge of God! How unfathomable are His judgments! And how untraceable are His ways!" Romans 11:33 Amplified Bible

Chapter One

January 7, 1984

"And we know that all things work together for good to those who love God, to those who are the called according to His purpose." Romans 8:28 - NKJV

The space heater kept the deer camp cabin warm even though the temperature stayed close to freezing outside all night. Deer season was over. Bill and Ron were the only ones at the hunting camp that weekend. Their deer blinds were several miles from the camp, amongst the hardwood trees in the Neches River bottom, a few miles north of Spurger, Texas. This part of the hunting lease was full of game. They planned on being in the woods by the crack of dawn. Those crafty squirrels would be out of their nests and scampering for something to eat at first light. They climbed out of their bunks and the aroma of hot coffee filled the camp. BeBe, Bill's four-legged baby, had been inside Bill's sleeping bag keeping his feet warm all night. She stayed cozy while the men drank their steaming cups of coffee. Bill finished his cup and pulled on his jacket. It was already getting pretty light in the east. He cranked the two three-wheelers and went back to the warmth of the camp while the ATVs warmed up. Bill put his thermos full of hot coffee and some snack cakes for breakfast in his backpack. He grabbed his shotgun and called to BeBe. Ron was already mounted on the three-wheeler he was riding that day as Bill shut the camp door. It was time to go hunting.

The ruts from the logging skidder made the road from the camp to the river bottom slow-going. That was okay with BeBe as she ran alongside the two three-wheelers, stopping occasionally to get a fresh sniff at the scent of a squirrel or rabbit that had crossed the road.

LOOK OUT SATAN ~ GOD'S AT WORK!

The guys finally made their way to the deer lease's old campsite. It was several miles from the current camp. Logging work had forced the men who leased the land for hunting to relocate their camp to its current location. Ron couldn't keep his three-wheeler running. The carburetor must have been gummed up. But now was not the time to worry about that. There was hunting to be done. Being a cop, Bill was careful not to give thieves any opportunity to steal his stuff. He pulled the ten-foot length of chain and a padlock from his backpack and chained the two ATVs to a tree. The old campsite was at the beginning of the hardwood where squirrels were more plentiful. The men loaded their shotguns, checked to make sure the weapons were on safety and walked down the logging road into the woods.

They had not walked far when they encountered the steep clay hill. The clay was slick for Bill and Ron even though the hunters wore hunting boots equipped with cleats. With a few slips and slides, the men made it down the two-hundred-plus feet of declining roadway until it finally leveled out. Now it was time for some serious hunting. As they slowly walked the logging road, their eyes were constantly scanning the nearby treetops for squirrels jumping from tree to tree, looking for nuts or seeds to feed on. BeBe was at a constant run, her nose two inches above the ground, sniffing all kinds of smells. She ran along the dirt road fifty yards or so ahead of the guys and then darted into the woods on a scent. She was having a blast.

The air was cold, but still. The men walked along the logging road, about two-hundred yards into the hardwood trees from the clay hill, when the leaves began rustling a few feet to their left. A squirrel, rustling leaves while looking for acorns, startled the men. At the same time, their presence startled the squirrel. The squirrel took off running behind them. Both men did an about-face as the squirrel ran alongside the road, trying to put distance between him and the two hunters. Safeties were taken off in an instant. Suddenly, the squirrel decided to turn left and ran across the road, forty feet away. Ron was to Bill's right and was the first to throw his Remington Model 1100

.12 guage semi-automatic shotgun to his shoulder. He fired and blew dust up from the road about a foot behind the squirrel which was now running in high gear. Bill knew to keep his eyes on the squirrel. He knew the squirrel would jump on a tree and scamper up it to find a limb to hide behind. He knew he must lock his eyes on that tree, or in an instant, all the trees would blend together and the squirrel would be gone. The squirrel found its tree and jumped three feet up the trunk, climbing as fast as possible. Bill's eyes were locked on the squirrel. He dared not even blink. He turned about a forty-five-degree angle and began walking toward the tree that was about thirty feet into the woods from the road.

Evidently, a grader had been down the logging road recently. Mounds of dirt about a foot high on either side of the road were evidence that the logging company had sent someone to grade the roads on the lease. Nature's elements, as well as heavy logging equipment, had a habit of wreaking havoc on these roads.

Bill had to step over the dirt mound as he reached it, bend down to go under the overhanging limbs, and keep his eyes on the tree the squirrel had climbed. Suddenly, the deafening sound of a shotgun blast pierced his ears. He was thrown forward by an unknown force as he was taking his third step from standing shoulder-to-shoulder with Ron. He fell to his knees and had to catch himself with his left hand to keep from being thrown face-first onto the ground. His right hand and forearm were suddenly in the most excruciating pain he'd ever felt in his life. His right forearm and hand felt as if they were on fire. Suddenly Ron was kneeling behind his friend, now supporting his back. "What happened?" Ron screamed as he looked down at his friend. "You shot me!" were the only words that could escape Bill's lips as his teeth were clenched from the searing pain.

How bad was the gunshot wound? Was he going to die in that river bottom? Bill forced himself to look. He could see a fragmented piece of bone, about a quarter-inch long, coming from the base knuckle of his right thumb. The rest of his thumb was gone. Blood was pouring, but not spurting from the wound. His right forearm was covered by his insulated underwear, long-sleeved shirt, and insulated jacket. He knew something was terribly wrong with his right forearm. It felt like someone had taken a white-hot piece of steel from a fire and stuck it to his forearm.

"My forearm, Ron! What's wrong with it?" Bill screamed in pain. His friend reached for the zipper and began to unzip the jacket. Instinctively, Bill grabbed the zipper with his left hand and zipped the zipper all the way to his throat. He didn't know why, at that moment, but he knew he had to keep the jacket on.

"Take your hunting knife and slit the sleeve, Ron. It's already blown to pieces," Bill told his friend. Ron unsheathed his fixed-blade hunting knife and gently slid it underneath the right webbed wrist of the sleeve. He pulled the wristband away from his friend's wrist, careful not to touch Bill with the knife. The sharp edge slowly cut into the jacket's material. More and more material was cut until Ron cut the sleeve all the way to the shoulder. He carefully pulled open the sleeve to expose a gash over six inches long on the inside of Bill's forearm. Bill looked, but just briefly, and could see the bloody muscles and ligaments exposed in his forearm. Bill knew he had to fight going into shock. The pain by itself was enough to make him go there. He also knew that looking at his wounds would hasten the onset of it. He wasn't dead yet. Somehow, some way, he was going to live.

"Ron, you've got to get me to a hospital," Bill told his friend. "I'm not dead yet. I'm not going to die here in this river bottom. Let's get me out of here!"

"Can you walk?" Ron asked, wondering if Bill could make it to the ATVs about a quarter-mile away.

"The pain's too bad," Bill replied. "Reach in my jeans pocket and get the keys to the three-wheeler and the padlock. Go get my three-wheeler and come back and get me," Bill instructed.

Ron was about to take off running when Bill called him back.

Bill's thinking wasn't very clear, but his survival instincts were off the chart. "Take your knife and cut a strip off my sleeve," Bill said.

"What for? I've got to hurry!" Ron exclaimed.

"I'm not dead, yet," Bill said. "And I'm not going to lay here and bleed to death while you're gone after the three-wheeler. Take that strip of sleeve and put it around my upper arm. If I start squirting blood, I can put one end of the strip in my mouth and the other end in my good hand. I can pull it tight enough to stop the blood from squirting. I'm not going to bleed to death down here in this river bottom," Bill declared again.

Ron removed his hunting knife from its sheath once again. Carefully he began to cut a strip from the torn sleeve, about two inches wide and the length of the sleeve from the wrist to the shoulder. He cut the sleeve very carefully, so as not to pull or jerk on Bill's injured arm and hand. When the strip was cut, Ron carefully wrapped it around Bill's right bicep and tied half a square knot in the front. He made sure one end would reach Bill's mouth and the other end was long enough for Bill's left hand. He hoped it wouldn't be needed.

With Bill tended to as best as possible, Ron took off running as hard as he could. Every second might be needed to save his friend's life, he thought. Shock was also hitting Ron, too. What happened? Had he really just shot his best friend? Denial at the moment was rampant.

BeBe knew something was wrong. Her master was lying on the ground. His friend was running and she started to run after him. Suddenly she realized her master was not running. She stopped and looked behind her. There he was, but her canine instincts told her something was wrong. She quickly turned around and ran back to Bill. She sniffed. She knew the smell of blood. Her dark brown eyes looked into her master's face. Something was definitely wrong. She had to help him.

Bill lay against his backpack. He wanted to close his eyes. But, wait! He had always been told if you are in shock and go to sleep, you might not wake up. He forced himself to keep his eyes open. He kept thinking, 'What happened?' He couldn't think clearly. The pain seemed to increase by the second. Was he going to make it? He had to. He wanted to see his six-month-old son again. He had to fight. Death would not win today. It was 7:15 a.m. He had been shot ten minutes ago. He was still alive.

It seemed forever, but it had only been a few minutes. Bill could hear the engine of the three-wheeler. Ron had the RPMs as high as they would go. He appeared around the curve in the road a few seconds later. Ron stopped beside his friend and dismounted, but kept the motor running. They had to hurry.

Ron gently reached to help Bill to his feet. But before he helped Bill get to his feet, his friend instructed, "Get the shotguns first."

"Forget the guns," Ron hollered, "We've got to hurry."

"I'm not leaving my gun for someone to steal," Bill retorted. "Jack the shells out of them and put them in the gun rack," Bill ordered. Hastily, Ron ejected all of the shotgun shells from both shotguns and placed them on the gun rack that was mounted in front of the handlebars of the three-wheeler. Ron then knelt down and gently put his arms under the arms of his friend. Slowly, Bill stood for the first time since being shot. He was woozy. He had lost a fair amount of blood, but he still wasn't spurting from an artery. Ron steadied his friend and then helped him take a couple of steps to the three-wheeler.

The Honda 110cc three-wheel ATV was going to have a load. It was built to carry one person, not two grown men. But, it would have to do. Just before deer season, Bill added a gun rack and an extra rack on the rear of his three-wheeler. He didn't have the money to buy one of those fancy racks that bolt behind the three-wheeler seat, so he sought the help of his father-in-law's friend, Lamar, who had a welding rig. Lamar gave Bill a list of materials needed to make a homemade rack. Bill bought the square tubing, expanded metal, washers, nuts, and bolts for the project. Bill and Lamar built his homemade rack the weekend before deer season began. Bill smiled with satisfaction as he looked at the rack mounted on the back of his three-wheeler. All he needed now was for deer season to begin, and a big ol' buck to walk into one of his shooting lanes. Little did he know at the time, the rack would not be for a deer – but for him!

As Ron helped Bill sit onto the homemade rack, Bill knew he had to keep his hand higher than his heart. Ron sat on the three-wheeler and gently started it toward the camp where Bill's truck would take them to a hospital. As Bill leaned onto his left elbow and had both feet on the right side of the three-wheeler, he put his right forearm over Ron's right shoulder. Bill knew this would help restrict the bleeding. In all his pain, Bill thought of his blood getting all over the front of Ron's clothes. 'Serves him right for shooting me,' Bill thought, almost smiling, but then he winced in pain as the three-wheeler hit a little bump in the road.

Suddenly the three-wheeler stopped. "We're at the clay hill," Ron said. Both men knew the problem without saying it. The 110cc three-wheeler was not going to get two grown men up that slippery hill. But, help was at the top of the hill and beyond.

"Let me off," Bill told Ron. Ron got off the three-wheeler and then helped his friend ease off the homemade rack and stand behind the ATV. 'It feels good to stand up, again,' Bill thought.

"I've got to keep my arm elevated," Bill told Ron. "You sit on the three-wheeler and push with your feet, and I'll be behind the three-wheeler pushing with my good hand and keep my right hand elevated on your shoulder," Bill instructed.

Ron accelerated the three-wheeler slowly. His friend was right behind the ATV and he had to be careful not to let it slide backward. True to form, the wet red East Texas clay started causing the three-wheeler to slip. Both men had traversed this hill numerous times, going to and from their deer blinds. It was always fun to slip and slide in the wet clay. This time, it was life and death. Bill pushed his hips against the back of the homemade rack to help Ron while steadying himself with his left hand and keeping his right hand on Ron's right shoulder. Ron dug both feet into the clay, trying to steady the three-wheeler from sliding. For a few seconds, it seemed the clay hill would win.

At the top of his lungs, Bill yelled, "GOD HELP US!" The three-wheeler steadied and slowly climbed the hill. At the top, Ron got off the ATV and helped Bill back onto the rack. With Bill's arm over Ron's shoulder and still dripping blood on the front of Ron's clothes, they slowly made it to the old campsite where Ron's 'dead' three-wheeler was still chained.

"Can you make it to the camp (the new camp)?" Ron asked Bill. It had been almost an hour since Bill had been shot. The pain was almost unbearable. Bill remembered how rough the logging road was between the old campsite and the current camp. There was no way he could stand the bouncing and jerking on that road.

"Leave me here," he told Ron. "You can make it much faster. Get my truck and come around to that gate." Bill pointed to a gate about three-hundred yards away on Hwy. 92. Ron took the shotguns off the gun rack and laid them on the ground beside Bill.

"I'll be back as quick as I can," Ron declared.

Bill's survival instincts were still at a peak. He had to think. He had to stay alive. "Hey, Ron, pour me a cup of coffee." Ron looked at his friend like he'd lost his mind. This was not the time to enjoy a cup of hot steaming coffee. Bill realized that hypothermia was also a very real enemy. The temperature was still in the thirties and he was lying on cold ground. Bill realized the heat from the coffee would raise his core body temperature and the coffee's caffeine would help him stay alert. He could not, he would not, let himself go to sleep.

Ron poured Bill a cup of coffee from the thermos. Steam rose from the cup. Bill sipped it, and it was 'soooo' good. Propped up on his backpack, Bill nodded to Ron and sarcastically said, "Don't take too long! And don't forget to chain my three-wheeler to a tree at camp!" Bill hollered.

BILL DAVIS

The three-wheeler roared down the road. In a few seconds, Bill couldn't even hear its motor. BeBe started to run after the three-wheeler. She thought Bill was on the ATV, as he had been a few moments ago. He whistled to her and she ran back to her master's side, again realizing something was still very wrong.

Bill drank his cup of black coffee, realizing for the second time since he'd been shot that he was alone, except for his trusty four-legged companion. His thinking was still foggy, but clearer than it had been. He reclined on his left side as he drank his coffee, but kept his right arm and hand resting on his right side. His injured hand was still higher than his heart. The tourniquet was still loosely tied around his right bicep. He knew he had to look one more time. Was this a bad dream or was it real? He raised his head from the backpack and looked at his right hand. The bone was still protruding from the base knuckle. His thumb was still gone. It wasn't hanging by a piece of skin or ligament. It wasn't there to be sewn back on once they got to a hospital. It was blown to smithereens. Dry blood covered the gaping wound and his hand. The jacket sleeve had fallen open and Bill could see his forearm. He could see the gaping wound and the bloody muscles. That was enough. He forced himself not to look.

As he lay on the ground, he slowly closed his eyes. His mind was racing. Surely with this kind of debilitating injury, his career in law enforcement was over. He couldn't bear the thought. His hand and arm were in excruciating pain, yet they felt numb. He felt like something was touching him; yet the pain was so immense, he couldn't really feel it. He slowly opened his eyes. There was his four-legged little girl. BeBe had eased beside him, had found his wounds, and was gently licking his hand. She was trying in her simple little way, to take care of her beloved master. Bill slowly pulled her away from licking his hand, and she gently lay beside him, keeping his chest warm.

Not only was BeBe there, but Jesus was there, too. Even as shock was creeping over him, Bill knew he was not alone. His prayer

LOOK OUT SATAN ~ GOD'S AT WORK!

was simple: "Father, if I've lost my thumb, don't let me lose my hand. But, if I've lost my hand, don't let me lose my arm. But, if I've lost my arm, don't let me lose my life." Bill didn't know what the future held, but the Lord did. He knew the Lord himself heard his prayer. It was time for another cup of hot, steaming black coffee.

Bill could see his truck. It was at the gate. Ron jumped out and was unlocking the gate. As it swung open, Ron was back in the truck and driving the three-hundred yards to his friend as quickly as possible. Bill held onto BeBe's collar. He had enough to deal with, without his precious little dog getting hit. Ron covered both Bill and BeBe with dust as he brought the truck to a halt. He was glad to see that his friend was still alive.

Ron ran to help Bill off the ground.

"Get the shotguns," Bill reminded him.

"To heck with the guns. We've got to get you to a hospital," Ron exclaimed. Bill was stubborn.

"I'm not dead yet, and I'm not going to die," Bill declared again. "Put those guns behind the seat."

Ron saw he was going to lose this argument, so he put both shotguns behind the truck seat.

"Okay, the guns are in the truck like you wanted. Now, get in the truck," Ron stated.

"Nope, now put my dog in the truck," Bill demanded. Ron reached down and picked up the little twenty-five-pound dog and put her in the passenger floorboard.

"Now, will you get in the truck?" the exasperated Ron asked.

"I thought you'd never ask," Bill stated with a wry sense of humor in such a desperate moment. Ron helped Bill to his feet and walked him the short distance to the passenger's side of the truck. Bill eased himself into the seat. Ron made sure Bill's injured arm was out of the way. As he started to shut the door, Bill reminded him to be sure and throw his backpack, that was still lying on the ground, into the bed of the truck. Ron grabbed the backpack and with a quick toss, threw it into the truck bed as he ran to the driver's side. In a moment, they were headed back to the gate.

Ron had left the gate open and the truck eased back to the highway. "Be sure and lock the gate," Bill reminded Ron, whose mind was only thinking of getting his friend to a hospital. Bill eased his left thumb into BeBe's collar as Ron opened the truck door to tend to the gate. In a second, Ron was back in the truck. The next stop – a hospital.

"Can you make it to Beaumont?" Ron asked. It had been over an hour-and-a-half since Bill had been shot. As hard as he was fighting it, he could feel the shock slowly taking over his body.

"I can't make it to Beaumont," Bill said. "Get me to Woodville." Bill knew that Woodville had a closer hospital. The medical staff could at least stabilize him and transport him later to a hospital in Beaumont. He had to have something for the pain, and soon!

Ron turned right, heading north on Hwy. 92. Both men knew that they could reach Hwy. 190, turn left, and be in Woodville in about twenty to thirty minutes.

Bill had to keep his injured hand and arm higher than his heart. He was weak and couldn't sit up in the seat. He laid to his left, putting his head on Ron's leg. He put his injured arm on his right side, thus keeping it higher than his heart. His left arm was outstretched; his left hand was holding BeBe by her collar. She was gently pulling forward as if wanting to get on the seat. When she rode with Bill, she always sat on the seat beside his right leg. Bill knew she probably wanted in her usual spot on the seat, but he couldn't bear the pain of her jumping on him. Suddenly, that quiet, small voice inside whispered, "Let her go." Bill didn't understand, but obeyed that quiet, small voice, and let go of BeBe's collar. Ever-so-gently, BeBe put first her left front paw, then her right front paw onto the seat. She then placed her left back paw, then her right back paw onto the seat. Very slowly she stretched her body prone, next to his, and laid her head on his outstretched left upper arm. Bill could feel her pressing her body next to his. She was taking care of her master. He gently stroked her head with his left hand. He swore, when it was her time to pass on, she would not do so alone. (He kept his promise.)

"A fork is coming up. A sign is showing it goes to Woodville. What should I do?" Ron declared. Bill was still lying on the seat but instinctively knew it was a farm-to-market road that was undoubtedly a shortcut by a few miles.

"Take it!" Bill hollered, hoping his instincts were right.

A few minutes later Ron declared, "We were right. We're at Hwy. 190. Woodville is only a couple of miles away."

Neither man knew where the hospital was located. As they entered the Woodville city limits, Ron pulled the truck into a service station. "My friend's been shot. We need a hospital," he yelled. Bill could hear a man giving directions, and Ron pulled the truck back onto the highway. The truck stopped and Bill could see the red light through the truck's windshield. "Where's a cop when you need one," Ron muttered, thinking a police officer might aid them in getting to the hospital with a police escort.

"Well, if the coast is clear, run the light and you just might find one," Bill retorted. With that, the truck suddenly made a left turn. Bill smiled as he saw the light was still red.

"We're here," Ron exclaimed as he made a right turn into the parking lot of the Tyler County Medical Center Hospital. He stopped the truck under the 'EMERGENCY' canopy. Bill eased his left thumb into BeBe's collar as Ron opened the driver's door and ran into the emergency room entrance door. Bill sat up in the seat. He couldn't believe it. They'd made it to the hospital. He looked at his watch. It was 9:05 a.m. Two hours had gone by.

Bill couldn't believe his eyes. He'd hoped for a gurney. Ron was accompanied by a nurse pushing a wheelchair. Oh, well. At least he wouldn't have to walk into the hospital.

Again, Bill reached for BeBe's collar. He knew she would bolt out the door as soon as it opened. Ron opened the passenger's door and said, "Come on, let's go."

"Nope, not until you reach in here and hold BeBe," Bill said.

"Quit worrying about the dang dog. Let's get you inside," Ron said.

"Nope, I'm not budging until you reach in here and hold my dog. I'm in no mood to chase after her right now," Bill declared defiantly. "And, you better get back out here with a bowl of water for her, too. Understood? And crack the windows a little, too, so she can have some fresh air," Bill stated to his friend.

With Bill's last statement, Ron looked at his friend and said, "I promise I will take good care of your dog." He replaced Bill's hand with his own in BeBe's collar.

"Okay, then. I'll go ahead and get out," Bill declared emphatically. He eased off the truck seat. The nurse held onto Bill's left arm and helped him ease into the wheelchair. As the nurse turned the wheelchair toward the emergency room door, Bill looked over his left shoulder to see Ron cracking the truck's windows about two inches. His little dog was being cared for. It was time to take care of him.

Bill has taken his program for children in grades Pre-K - 5th grade and transformed it into coloring book form.

He enjoys autographing his coloring book to children with a hand-printed message and signature.

The next page is the cover of the coloring book.

The following four pages are the pages he devoted to gun safety.

Child Safety

First & Forever With Officer Bill

By: Sgt. Bill Davis
Illustrated by: Delbert Kerr

Grown-ups sometimes play with real guns. This is WRONG!!! When this happens, sometimes people get hurt and even killed. Many years ago, Officer Bill and a friend were hunting. His friend was not careful with a real gun and he accidentally shot Officer Bill.

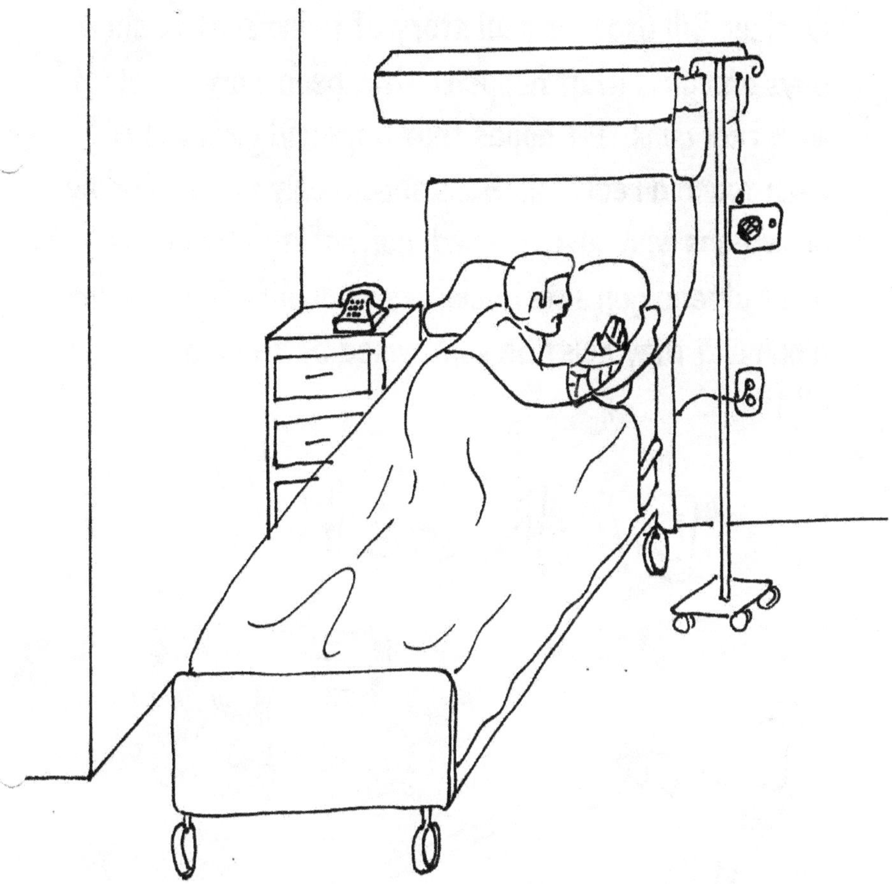

Officer Bill was taken to the hospital. His thumb and arm were injured.

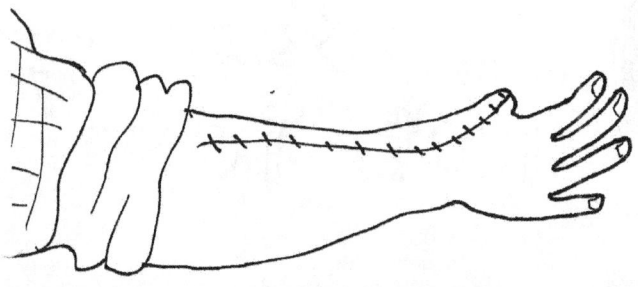

Officer Bill uses his real story of being shot to show boys and girls what happens when people are careless with real guns. He hopes that boys and girls will not even touch a real gun. Guns should only be handled by grown-ups who have learned gun safety. Students must attend gun safety classes to qualify for shooting a gun and they must be supervised by trained adults at all times.

One of the tools Officer Bill carries is a gun. Is it a real gun or a play gun?

      Real gun____ Play gun____

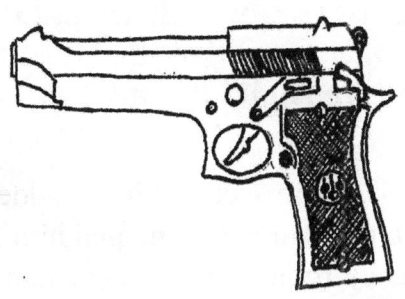

Is a water gun a real gun? Yes No

Is a BB gun a real gun? Yes No

Is a pellet gun a real gun? Yes No

Should boys and girls ever touch a real gun, especially if Mom or Dad is not present? Yes No

Should you tell a grown-up if you see someone with a gun?   Yes No

Chapter Two

Hospitals, Doctors, & Nurses

"The angel of the Lord encamps all around those who fear Him, and delivers them. Oh, taste and see that the Lord is good; Blessed is the man who trusts in Him!" Psalms 34:78 KJV

Five of God's angels, all dressed in white, suddenly appeared to take care of Bill. Two of them gently helped him from the wheelchair and onto the emergency room gurney. They had to get those bloody clothes off of him and see the seriousness of his wounds. Armboards were placed on both sides of the gurney. One nurse had a pair of scissors and began cutting the bloody insulated jacket, shirt, long-johns top, and t-shirt off. Bill felt someone doing something to his hunting boots. He looked down and observed one of the nurses with another pair of scissors, about to cut his boots off.

"Ma'am, don't cut those boots. They don't even belong to me. They belong to the city of Beaumont. They're my SWAT boots," Bill exclaimed. "I'm not shot in the foot." With that, she unlaced his boots. The half-inch cut her scissors made was a reminder of the day Bill almost lost his boots and his life. The boots lasted him another four years on the SWAT team. Then, the scissor-happy nurse started to cut his just-broke-in, five-year-old pair of Levi jeans. "Ma'am," Bill said, "Please don't cut my good jeans. Undo them and I'll lift my butt off this gurney and you can slide them off of me." She did as he asked. The Levi's lasted him another ten years.

One of the nurses was beside his left arm and another nurse was beside his right arm. As they began to gently cut away the upper garments, Bill began to break out in a sweat. A fifth nurse, an older woman with a kind and gentle face, began to wipe his face with a cold, damp towel. It felt so good.

The next item to come off was the underwear. The nurse with the scissors attending to the lower half of his body took care of them with two quick cuts. The nurses gently sat Bill up on the gurney for just a second and removed the upper clothing from his back that had been cut away in the front.

"Why can't I keep my underwear?" Bill asked. One of the nurses looked at him and told him that some of the shotgun pellets had somehow ended up in his abdomen. They didn't know to what extent his abdominal injuries might be. They didn't know if any of his organs, including his intestines, had been injured, or if he was bleeding internally.

'Wow!' Bill thought. He didn't know that he was injured in the abdomen. The pain in his right hand and forearm was very intense. He had not even noticed that he'd been shot in the abdomen, too.

Ron eased into the emergency room, careful not to get in the way of the nurses that were tending to his friend. "BeBe has fresh air and a fresh bowl of water," Ron proclaimed to his friend.

Both Baptist Hospital and St. Elizabeth Hospital in Beaumont had helicopters. As the nurses attended to Bill, he began to think of how to get to one of the hospitals in Beaumont. A helicopter ride would be less than thirty minutes. An ambulance ride would be about forty-five minutes to an hour. The helicopter ride would get him to a Beaumont hospital quicker. But he and Ron had gone to the hunting camp in HIS truck with HIS dog. Instead of worrying about himself, Bill was worried about his friend, his dog, and his truck. Ron was still very upset, and rightfully so. He shot his best friend. It was an accident. Bill knew that. But, Bill knew that Ron, in his state of mind, might end up in Lufkin instead of Beaumont if Bill took the helicopter and left Ron to get to Beaumont on his own. Bill also knew that if he took the ambulance, the ride might take a few minutes longer, but Ron could follow the ambulance in HIS truck with HIS dog. Following an ambulance might be the better option, Bill thought.

BILL DAVIS

"Find my jeans and get my police commission wallet," Bill asked. Ron returned a few minutes later, holding the leather police commission holder. "Look behind my commission," Bill instructed, "and you will find a SWAT team list. Call Joe." (Crutchfield, a.k.a. 'Little Heat' – a Beaumont P.D. captain and the B.P.D. SWAT team's commander at that time. Joe was also on the same hunting lease with Bill and Ron.). "Tell him what has happened. Tell him I need a police escort for my ambulance from here to St. Elizabeth (hospital)." With that, Ron went to find a phone.

Someone suddenly grabbed Bill's privates. 'What, now?' he thought. The wonderful nurse was still wiping his face and upper body with the damp cloth. Bill raised his head slightly to look and see what was going on in the direction of his groin. All the nurses attending to him appeared to be middle-aged female nurses. Most had probably been nurses their entire working career. But the one who was now attending to his private area was a young, beautiful, nurse with blonde hair, blue eyes, and very shapely. "Now just relax, Mr. Davis," she said as she inserted the catheter into his body. Bill looked up at the ceiling and took a deep breath. It was time to pray again. 'Lord, please, don't let me lose control,' he thought. Once again, God answered his prayer.

The doctor at the emergency room finally came in. It was easy to see that he was of Asian ancestry. Bill later found out that his regular medical practice was in Fort Worth. He came to rural hospitals a couple of weekends a month to help out in emergency rooms. The nurses had wiped away most of the dried blood from Bill's abdomen, right forearm, and hand.

"You need an orthopedic surgeon," the doctor declared. "Where are you from?" the doctor inquired. "Beaumont," Bill replied. "They'll have one (an orthopedic surgeon) on call," the doctor declared. He gave the nurses some medical orders and left the room. He was having his nurses prepare Bill for his ambulance ride to Beaumont.

One of the nurses began covering his wounds with Betadine.

LOOK OUT SATAN ~ GOD'S AT WORK!

Gauze was then gently placed over his wounds. More gauze was used to lightly wrap around his hand and arm. An ace bandage was then lightly wrapped from his fingertips to his elbow. Another nurse left for a few minutes then returned. "Roll to your right, Mr. Davis," she said. "I have something for you that's going to make you feel much better. It'll be a big stick, but then you'll start feeling better in a few minutes." Bill was about to feel the wonderful effects of Demerol.

Another nurse hung a saline bag on the gurney pole. Bill asked about the smaller bag on the pole going into his I.V. It was antibiotics. He thought he'd lost a lot of blood. Where was the bag of blood to replenish all of the blood he'd lost? (He'd find out later how God took care of his blood supply.)

Ron returned to Bill's gurney and advised that he'd gotten in touch with Joe Crutchfield. "He's taking care of the police escort for you," Ron advised. "I also called my house," Ron continued. Bill's wife, Jan, and six-month-old son, Dusty, had spent the night with his wife, Betty Ann, and their girls. Jan and Betty Ann were best friends. "They're going to meet us at St. Elizabeth Hospital," Ron explained.

Bill was beginning to finally relax. The pain was not gone, but the Demerol was starting to work. It was taking some of the edge off the searing pain. The catheter nurse told Bill, "Just relax when you need to pee." He looked at her inquisitively. He didn't want to have an 'accident' in his bed. "We need to see if there's blood in your urine," and she explained about the urine collection bag just below Bill's bed. He was still learning about the catheter.

"Oh my God," the deputy said as he looked into Bill's face. He saw the uniform of a Tyler County Deputy Sheriff and a face that he didn't recognize. But, the deputy definitely recognized the face of the veteran Beaumont Police Department child abuse detective. The deputy possibly recognized Bill from being on television many times discussing a particular investigation on the evening news, or a local TV talk show building awareness with the viewing audience about child abuse and child molestation. Bill also worked on investigations that took him into Tyler County. Bill also started presenting child abuse seminars about six months earlier and the deputy may have been in the audience at one of Bill's first seminars.

"I need a little help, brother," the detective said to the deputy. "Can you help get my ambulance to Beaumont a little quicker?"

"You just relax," the deputy told his brother officer. "I'll have you there in no time at all. Your escort is set up for you all the way to the hospital." Bill took a deep breath, realizing that it was (and is) such an honor to be a part of the law enforcement fraternity and the 'thin blue line.' Bill and Ron had been at the hospital for about an hour-and-a-half when the ambulance personnel arrived to transport Bill to Beaumont. "I didn't know our patient was going to be Sgt. Bill Davis," one of the attendants exclaimed. Bill didn't know them, but they evidently knew the child abuse detective from Beaumont. They went about their duties, getting everything ready to get Bill into their ambulance. One of the nurses came into the room with another shot. "Roll a little to your right," she instructed. "This'll make your ambulance ride a little easier." Thank God for Demerol.

The male ambulance attendant drove the ambulance a little faster than normal, keeping up with the deputy that was ahead, clearing the way for the ambulance. The female paramedic attended to Bill in the back of the ambulance, making sure his vitals were strong and he was making the trip with no problems. Bill raised his head and could see the trees along the roadside going by pretty fast. His truck with Ron at the wheel was following the ambulance.

"I need a cigarette," Bill declared. He could see the pack of cigarettes in the lady paramedic's shirt pocket.

"You can't smoke in the ambulance. We have oxygen on board," she said.

"Ma'am, we're going to be at the hospital in a few minutes. They're not going to let me smoke in the emergency room. Then, they're going to take me to surgery. Please let me have just one. I'd give one to you if the roles were switched," he pleaded. The attendant couldn't stand it.

"Don't you tell a soul or my butt's mud," she said as she reached into her pocket and got a cigarette. She placed it in his mouth and lit it. He took a deep drag and savored the smoke as he inhaled it. He thumped his ashes in her palm until the cigarette was finished. She extinguished it for him. She shouldn't have let him have it. But, she was glad she could help comfort him a little. (Bill would kick the habit in January 1991.)

Looking out the back of the ambulance window doors, Bill could see that Ron was still behind them. Occasionally the paramedic driving the ambulance would use his siren to get cars to get out of the way or as they were approaching an intersection. He could hear a second siren and knew one of his law enforcement comrades was still up front, leading the way. Bill later learned that the Tyler County Sheriff's deputy escorted his ambulance through Tyler County. As they entered Hardin County, the deputy gave way, and a Texas Department of Public Safety Highway Patrol Trooper took over the escort role. Bill occasionally looked up as the ambulance slowed, approaching various intersections.

Southbound on Hwy. 69 took the emergency caravan through Kountze. South of Kountze, the highway continued through the western part of Lumberton. The caravan continued through Lumberton, sirens blaring. South of Lumberton, Hwy. 69 merged with U.S. Hwy. 96. At the Pine Island Bayou Bridge, the boundary between Hardin County and Jefferson County, and the beginning of the Beaumont city limits, the DPS trooper gave way. A Beaumont Police Department officer now led the way for Bill. He later learned the driver of the B.P.D. police car was Officer Becky Crossland.

The ambulance made a left turn and Bill could tell, as he looked out the ambulance doors that they were turning onto North Street. Shortly after making the turn, the siren went silent. St. Elizabeth Hospital was less than one-hundred yards away. Bill had come to the hospital hundreds of times. Many of those times were while he was a patrol officer from June 1972 to October 1977. Many of those hospital visits were to see victims of various crimes, especially child physical abuse and child sexual molestation victims, starting in October 1977. He knew the nurses and doctors that worked there. They had worked on the medical end of many of his child abuse investigations. Now, they were about to work on him. He was the one on the gurney, not someone else.

The ambulance doors opened. The first faces Bill saw were his brother-in-law, Danny Rawlinson, and his father-in-law, Herman Rawlinson. Behind them were Beaumont P.D. Captain David Ivey and Captain Joe Crutchfield. Jan and Betty Ann were beside the four men. Several other Beaumont P.D. officers surrounded Bill's gurney as the paramedics slowed to a halt for everyone to greet their fallen relative and colleague. Jan was holding Bill's pride and joy, his little boy. Dusty's and Bill's eyes met. The toddler was happy to see his daddy. He reached for his daddy and they touched. Emotions flooded Bill as he touched his son's hand and then his face with his left hand. Bill and Jan had been on the Edna Gladney Adoption Center's adoption list for eighteen months before they were finally rewarded with a beautiful six-day-old little boy. Only a few hours earlier, Bill had wondered if he'd ever see his six-month-old son again. Slobber drooled from Dusty's mouth onto Bill's hand and face. He was teething. The paramedics told the concerned friends and family they needed to get Bill into a room. They could visit as soon as he was settled. Dusty began to cry as they rolled his daddy away. Bill didn't wipe his hand or face.

The nurses in the emergency room began to attend to their new patient. This patient wasn't just another patient. He was a friend, someone they knew. He was a man who had put his life on the line for many people. Now, his life was on the line. The nurses and paramedics transferred Bill from the ambulance gurney to an emergency room gurney. The bags of saline and antibiotics were hung on the gurney pole. The paramedics had their papers signed. The care of their patient was officially transferred to the hospital. They said their goodbyes and Bill thanked them for taking care of him. He winked at the female paramedic as he thanked her. He wasn't flirting. It was his way of thanking her, again, for the cigarette. The secret was safe with him.

The nurses gently cut away Bill's bandages, exposing his raw wounds. "I always enjoy visiting with you when you come to the E.R.," Dr. Herman Gerhardt said as he looked down at his friend and new patient. "But, I really didn't want to visit you like this," the doctor explained. He looked at Bill's wounds, surveying the damage.

Captains Crutchfield and Ivey had stayed in the room. "Doc, I know the exact location on the deer lease where he got shot," Joe said. "If it's not too late, I'll drive to the lease, find his thumb, and get back here for you to sew it on."

"The time frame wouldn't matter," the doctor explained. "It was a shotgun blast. His thumb's blown to smithereens." Doc always had a way with words.

"We'll get hold of the ortho on call," Dr. Gerhardt explained. "We'll get you into surgery as quickly as possible." "Let's get x-rays of his hand and abdomen," Dr. Gerhardt instructed one of the nurses. With that, he turned and left. He had other patients to attend to. The nurses gently covered Bill's wounds again.

Nurses constantly checked on Bill to make sure his vital signs were stable and he was as comfortable as possible. Everyone was waiting on the orthopedic surgeon.

Jan brought Dusty into Bill's emergency room. The little man was wearing his red, white, and blue long-sleeve outfit. He started waving his arms and jabbering as he saw his daddy again. Jan helped hold Dusty as she put him on Bill's chest. His little hands caressed his daddy's face as he drooled all over Bill's face and neck. Everything was going to be okay.

Ron came in to check on his friend. "How's my dog?" was

BILL DAVIS

Bill's first question. "She's at your house, with food and water," Ron explained. That was one worry off Bill's mind. That dog was one of those dogs you have once in a lifetime. She was special.

One of Bill's nurses came in with a Demerol shot and advised everyone he needed to rest. A couple of hours later, a new doctor gently awoke his patient. He was tall and lanky, but with a caring smile. "I'm Dr. Mickey Smith, your orthopedic surgeon," the doctor explained. Nurses removed Bill's bandages once again. Dr. Smith carefully looked at Bill's forearm and where his thumb used to be. He also looked at Bill's abdomen. "You're lucky," Dr. Smith told Bill. "The pellets in your abdomen are in the muscle tissue and did not touch any of your organs or intestines. As soon as I can get a surgical team together, we'll get you into surgery."

Still not wanting to face reality, Bill asked, "Is my thumb gone, Doc?" "I'm afraid it is," Dr. Smith replied. "But the good news is, we're going to save your hand. It'll be a while, but you should be able to have full use of your hand with only a short thumb." Dr. Smith had a kind and reassuring face. Dr. Smith turned and left the room. He had a team to assemble. Bill closed his eyes, savoring Dr. Smith's good news. 'Thank you, Lord,' Bill thought, and let the Demerol do its job.

"Mr. Davis, wake up," one of his nurses said as she gently awoke her patient. "You'll be going to surgery in a few minutes. "You might want to visit with your family before you go." He wanted to see everyone, especially his son. The nurse left. A few minutes later, the room was filled with officers, friends, and relatives. Dusty had to give his daddy another slobbery kiss. It was time to go to surgery. Bill noticed the clock. It was 1:00 p.m. It had been six hours.

He slowly came back to consciousness. He was so thirsty and his throat was sore. Jan and Betty Ann took turns feeding Bill ice bits. His hand and arm were heavily bandaged. As the anesthesia wore off, Bill learned that Dr. Smith had debrided and sewn up most of the wound to his thumb. An opening was left at the tip of what was now a nub. Bill would learn the reason his thumb had not been completely sewn up at a later time. The gash to his forearm would need more attention. Dr. Smith had checked inside the wound and was quite amazed. There were seventeen #6 shotgun pellets in Bill's forearm. The skin was completely gone, leaving an open wound approximately six inches by two inches. The muscles had been damaged but would heal. It did not appear that any of the leaders for the joints in his fingers that ran through his forearm had been cut. That in itself was a miracle. Dr. Smith could have performed a skin graft on the forearm, but he decided to wait a few days. If the swelling in the forearm went down, he might be able to take Bill back into surgery and pull his skin over the open wound, stitching it tightly, without having to do a graft. Time would tell.

The next five days passed slowly. The Demerol shots helped dull the pain, although it never went away. Bill began learning how to use his left hand for everything – eating, drinking, and using his toothbrush, to name just a few simple things. Friends and relatives came and went. Bill awoke one afternoon and saw one of his uniformed African-American colleagues standing at the foot of his bed. As his eyes focused, he saw the big white-toothed grin of his fellow officer and SWAT teammate, Al Johnson. Suddenly, it was like someone turned on a light bulb in Bill's mind. He had done so many things to keep himself alive until he reached the hospital in Woodville. Many of the survival techniques he utilized were a mystery and instinctive at the time, but they worked. Al was a medic in the military. He'd been to Vietnam. Many times at SWAT training when there was inclement weather, the SWAT members would train indoors.

Sometimes the training consisted of Al teaching his teammates life-saving medical techniques. Some of those techniques were how to keep a fellow teammate alive if they were shot on a SWAT callout, and how to keep that teammate alive until he could be carried to paramedics on the outer perimeter of a SWAT situation. Bill suddenly

realized that everything he did that kept him alive on that river bottom had been taught by Al Johnson in those SWAT training sessions.
("Thanks, once again, Al!")

Bill's hospital phone was close enough that he could answer it himself. It rang, and he answered, "Hello." "Officer Davis, this is Chief Bauer. I wanted to call and check on you." It was Chief Willie Bauer, himself. He was a legend. He'd been the police chief longer than any other police chief with the city of Beaumont. When you met Chief Bauer in a hallway, you always spoke. He usually replied with, "Officer, how are you?" He never called you by name.

Now he had not only called, but for the first time in Bill's almost twelve years with the police department, the chief had actually called him by name. The two men talked for several minutes with the chief asking about the accident and how things were going. The conversation ended with Chief Bauer telling Bill to call him if he needed anything – that he (Bill) had a straight line to his office. Bill thanked the chief for his words of encouragement and hung up. It was a telephone call that Chief Bauer didn't have to make, but he did. Bill would never forget it.

There was one nurse's aide that Bill would never forget. While hooked up to an I.V. and the catheter, he couldn't get out of bed. He had not been able to take a shower to feel somewhat clean. Some nurses would come in and wash his face, arms, back, and feet. They would hand him a wet washcloth to wash the rest of his body. Sometimes he would and sometimes he was hurting so bad, he didn't feel like it. This wonderful lady always came in with a smile on her face. Her dark skin radiated her beautiful white teeth. She got her warm bowl of water and washed his hair. She cleaned his face and continued down the rest of his body. She never handed the washcloth to him but did her duty to give her patient a bath. She dried him off, rubbed him down with baby powder, and replaced his old hospital gown with a clean one. He felt clean and alive. She was truly one of

God's angels that made hurting people feel better.

Tests on Bill's urine further showed his organs and bowels were okay. Bill's nurse for that shift came into his room and advised it was time to remove the catheter. He had kind of gotten used to it, peeing when he felt like it and not having to get out of bed or use one of those urine pitchers. "Just relax," she said. 'Yeah, right,' he thought. He'd heard that one before. She slowly removed the tiny tube that felt like she was pulling a garden hose through his body. A few seconds later and another ordeal was over, or so he thought. A couple of hours later, the nurses could hear him down at the nurse's station screaming as he urinated for the first time without the catheter. No one warned him how bad it would burn the first few times he urinated after the tube had been removed. It was another one of those experiences he would never forget.

Thursday, January 12, was the day Dr. Smith scheduled Bill's second surgery. As Bill was wheeled toward the operating room he was greeted by Dr. Smith and one of Bill's friends, Mike Ramsey. Mike was a former police officer. He went to law school and was now an attorney with a local law firm. He'd come to see his friend during Bill's five-day recuperation in the hospital. Mike had not been retained as an attorney. But as Bill's friend, he suggested that photos of his injuries be taken while the bandages were removed before surgery. At Bill's request, Mike was going to provide the camera, and Dr. Smith agreed to take the photos with Mike's camera and then hand the camera back to Mike outside the operating room. After saying hello to the two men, the nurses wheeled Bill's gurney into the operating room. The nurses were busy preparing for the surgery. A man introduced himself as Bill's anesthesiologist and asked him a series of questions. Bill looked forward to being put under anesthesia and feeling no pain.

The doctor started the anesthesia. Bill waited. He didn't even start counting backward from one hundred. He just waited to feel the anesthetic feeling rush over him. Suddenly his veins were on fire. It felt like liquid fire was being poured into his body. He sat up on the operating table screaming at the top of his lungs. "Oh God, I'm on fire!" he screamed over and over. One nurse tried to hold him down on the operating table, then two, then three. Four nurses and five seconds later, the anesthesia took over as Bill collapsed on the table. Dr. Smith explained to Mike that the antibiotics that Bill was being given intravenously had irritated his veins. The cold anesthesia entered Bill's raw and irritated veins and was evidently somewhat uncomfortable. (That was an understatement.)

Bill slowly awakened from his second surgery in less than a week. His right arm was heavily bandaged again. But this time, his wrist was bent toward the inside of his forearm as far as it would go. He tried to straighten it but the heavy bandages prevented him from moving it. The nurses explained that Dr. Smith was able to remove debris and close his wound without having to do a skin graft. But in not using a skin graft, Dr. Smith had to stretch Bill's existing skin as tight as it could stretch, thus pulling his hand forward. He would have to work on straightening it in therapy.

Chapter Three

Aftercare

"The steps of a good man are ordered by the Lord, and He delights in his way." Psalms 37:23 - NKJV

Sunday, January 15, 1984, eight days after being shot, Bill returned home. Wow! It felt good to be out of that hospital bed and back in his recliner. It was refreshing to sit and watch Dusty crawl and play with his toys which were scattered on the living room floor.

Lt. Harold Engstrom came by to visit his friend. He was Bill's lieutenant while he was in the patrol division. At one time, Bill had given his two-week notice to the Beaumont Police Department. He went through all of the testing for a smaller department in the area. On the last day of the two-week notice, at 3:00 p.m. and with the resignation to take effect at 5:00 p.m., Harold talked his patrol officer and friend into pulling the resignation. It was a move Bill would never regret. Harold was now Bill's lieutenant in the Special Crimes Unit. Bill opened the front door for his friend. As Harold entered the living room, he had to move some of Dusty's toys out of the way to sit on the couch. "I'm sorry Dusty's toys are scattered everywhere," Bill said.

Harold turned to his friend and made a remark Bill would never forget: "Don't ever apologize for him and his toys. It shows your house is a home."

Harold also brought a package of venison backstrap. He knew Bill had not killed a deer that year. It would sure be tasty when Jan 'chicken-fried' it.

Mike Ramsey also came by a few days after Bill arrived home from the hospital. He wanted to check on his friend. He also knew that even though Bill had medical insurance, his part of the bills would be astronomical. In conversation, Mike suggested that Bill think about suing Ron. Bill wouldn't hear of it. The shooting had been an accident. Mike was merely explaining some of Bill's available options without increasing the financial burden on his family. These options were something Bill had not thought of. Bill made it perfectly clear to Mike that he would not go forward with this idea if Ron was not one-hundred-percent for it. His friendship with Ron was priceless and he would not jeopardize that under any circumstances. There were some things that money could not buy, and his friendship with Ron was one of those things. Bill asked if Mike would meet together with him and Ron and explain the legalities of a suit. Mike agreed.

The meeting took place a few days later. Still acting as a friend, Mike explained all of the legalities to Bill and Ron. To Bill's surprise, Ron was all for the lawsuit. A few days later, after careful consideration, Bill asked Mike to represent him. Not long afterward, Mike filed the lawsuit against Ron's homeowner's insurance policy. This lawsuit would not put a financial burden on Ron and his family.

Jan worked for the Jefferson County Sheriff's Department as a corrections officer in the county jail. Having accrued sick-leave days with the department that could be used for herself, or for an immediate family member, she was able to take off from work the entire eight days that Bill was confined to the hospital. When Bill was able to return home, Jan went back to work the following day. Bill's mother-in-law, Mary Rawlinson, came every day and took care of Bill and Dusty. Bill really enjoyed his days of quality time with his son. Mary, affectionately known as 'MeMe,' always tried to arrive shortly after Jan left for work at 6:30 a.m. One day, she was running a little late. That was not a big deal until Dusty awoke a little earlier than usual. Instead of being in the normal jovial mood, Dusty started crying. As Bill started to pick his son up with his left hand, he smelled it. Dusty had a 'poopy' diaper. 'Oh, well,' Bill thought, 'MeMe will be here any moment.' He tried to entertain his son but nothing worked. Dusty wanted out of that stinking diaper. His son was now screaming. Bill laid Dusty down on the bed. He held his legs up by the back of his right forearm, hoping Dusty wouldn't kick him on one of his wounds and break his stitches. The poop was everywhere. It was probably the worst diaper Dusty had ever had in his little life. The diaper was so full. Poop was running down Dusty's legs. With his son's legs high in the air, Bill undid the diaper. God had added an extra bit of aroma, Bill thought as he managed to remove the loaded diaper. Dusty stopped crying and was now making all kinds of noises. He was being tended to. Dusty was finally wiped clean and the new diaper was finally in place. Still weak from being shot, Bill was covered in sweat from the ordeal. MeMe arrived just as the stinky ordeal ended. It was a diaper change to be remembered forever.

Wednesday, January 18, was Bill's first post-op visit to Dr. Smith's Office. It was time to remove the stitches from the thumb area of his hand. The nurse unwrapped and cut away Bill's bandages. He immediately noticed that these stitches were not ordinary stitches. They looked about the size of trotline string. The nurse explained that it was necessary for Dr. Smith to use the largest sutures available in order to pull the skin together and hold it together to heal.

"Why did Dr. Smith leave an opening in the top of my thumb and at the end of my forearm scar?" Bill asked. The nurse explained that a lot of fibers from the insulated jacket he was wearing were forced inside his arm by the shotgun pellets. These fibers were foreign objects and his body would reject them. His body would force these fibers from his body and needed an opening for the fibers to be removed. He kind of understood, but he would learn more about this soon enough.

On Monday, January 23, Bill returned to Dr. Smith's office. It was time to have the stitches in his forearm removed. The same nurse slowly snipped the stitches and removed them. "I need to warn you about something," she said. Bill thought, 'Oh, no, now what – an infection or something like that?' She explained, with most traumatic incidents, emotions build up inside a person. "You're going to explode one day," she explained. "You're going to come unglued and when it happens, there's nothing you can do about it. Just let it come out, and then you can get on with healing." He listened, but thought (just like a typical man), 'Not me. I can handle this. I'm in control. What she's describing may happen to others, but not to me.'

Dr. Smith looked at the healing wounds. The stitches were removed only moments before. "I was worried that your skin would die due to the trauma it suffered and the stitches would not hold," he said. "But, everything is looking good." That was reassuring, Bill thought. "We're going to start your therapy today," Dr. Smith explained. "I'm also going to refer you to a doctor in New Orleans. He's the best hand surgeon in the world and you're going to need some reconstructive surgery." Bill later learned that Dr. Smith had studied under this world-renowned doctor and had the utmost respect for him.

Before Dr. Smith left the room to visit another patient, Bill had to ask the doctor a question that had been nagging at him for weeks. "Doctor, my thumb was blown off and arteries to my thumb were torn open. Why did I not spurt blood when I got shot?" Bill asked. Dr. Smith patiently explained to Bill that the arteries to his thumb were not neatly cut like with a knife or a saw blade. Dr. Smith said that an artery cut smoothly would have caused him to spurt blood. But with Bill's situation, the fibers of the artery had been jaggedly ripped apart. In a life-saving act, the artery's fibers clung to each other which closed off the majority of the blood in the artery. Dr. Smith told Bill he still oozed blood from his wounds but did not spurt blood. Bill never needed a blood transfusion. Bill exited Dr. Smith's clinic thanking God once again for saving his life.

The therapy department was in the same building and around the corner from the doctor's offices at the orthopedic clinic. Bill walked up to the reception desk and handed the lady the papers he'd gotten from Dr. Smith. The papers held Dr. Smith's instructions as to what Bill needed to begin therapy. "Have a seat and Penny will be right with you," the lady advised. A few minutes later, Bill met another angel from God. He didn't realize it at the time, but he would a year later.

She was beautiful and had a pleasant smile. "Hello, Bill. I'm Penny. Let's get started," she proclaimed but talking in a most unusual accent. "Where are you from?" Bill asked. "Australia," she replied.

Bill sat in a chair beside Penny's desk. His arm rested on a blue piece of thick foam rubber at about a thirty-degree angle. Penny gently removed Bill's bandages and surveyed the damage. "Let's start with the whirlpool," she said. With that, she sat Bill beside the stainless steel vat with the 'outboard motor' apparatus attached to it. Bill eased his arm up to his elbow in the warm water and Penny turned on the whirlpool motor. 'Hey, this therapy isn't too bad,' Bill thought. Little did he know what was yet to come.

Penny turned off the motor after about fifteen minutes and then gently towel-dried Bill's hand and arm. They went back to Penny's desk and he rested his arm on the blue foam. With a pair of tweezers in her hand, Penny began concentrating on the small one-half-inch open wound at the end of Bill's nub. Slowly, she began to remove tiny pieces of insulation that his body had pushed to the opening. This process would make up the first thirty minutes of Bill's therapy for months to come.

The pain from the shotgun blast to Bill's thumb and forearm overshadowed the pain from the shotgun pellets in his abdomen. His forearm, wrist, hand, and fingers were immobilized from the time he reached the Woodville hospital until his stitches were removed. He noticed his wrist was hurting but he assumed it was from keeping it immobilized. As Penny gently tried to move Bill's wrist, acute pain wrenched through his wrist and hand. His wrist was sprained. When the shotgun blast hit him, the pellets blew away his thumb, which was on the inside of his grip to his own shotgun. The four pellets that entered Bill's abdomen ricocheted off the metal housing of his shotgun and into his abdomen. One pellet entered the tip of Bill's middle finger and exited through the fingernail. Another pellet also entered the tip of his index finger and also exited through the fingernail. The force of the shotgun blast kicked Bill's shotgun outward, causing the stock of his gun to sprain his wrist. The sprain would cause Bill's therapy to go more slowly. The wrist needed to heal before he could perform any twisting and turning with his hand.

Penny worked with Bill to get some mobility back into his fingers and wrist. After the whirlpool and insulation plucking session, the exercises would start slowly. The exercises were to move each joint of each finger, move his wrist, and stretch the skin of his forearm. Bill was going to have some large scars from his wounds. She worked intently to massage and soften the inflamed scar tissue. On one of Bill's first days in therapy, Penny produced a clear gel and started applying it to Bill's nub. "What is that?" Bill asked. "Silicone," Penny responded, "the kind that is used for breast implants." She molded the silicone around Bill's nub. She blended an accelerant with the silicone to cause it to harden into a rubbery substance. It was almost like he had his own silicone glove for his nub. She did the same thing to his forearm scar. She explained that his hand and nub would stay wrapped with an ace bandage for weeks. The silicone coverings would massage the scar tissue, making it softer and easier to respond to therapy. She also produced finger splints that applied constant pressure to Bill's bent fingers. These splints would slowly straighten Bill's fingers. They were extremely painful and he could only wear them a few minutes at a time. He was learning very quickly that therapy 'ain't' for sissies.

During the second week of therapy, Penny produced a gripping object that would measure the strength in his hand. Bill placed it in his good hand and squeezed. Lifting weights for years gave his hand greater-than-average strength. It took some manipulating but he was able to get the gripper into his injured hand. "Okay, squeeze as hard as you can," Penny said. Bill squeezed until he was shaking. He squeezed the gripper as hard as he could. He knew the results would not be good. "Well how bad is it?" he asked Penny. Sympathetically she looked at her patient and stated, "The needle never moved."

Bill's appointment with Dr. Dan Riordan in New Orleans was set for Valentine's Day, February 14, 1984. Mike Ramsey filed the lawsuit against Ron's homeowner's insurance. It had been five weeks since the shooting and Bill was going to therapy on Mondays, Wednesdays, and Fridays. He was getting stronger and the pain wasn't as constant. However, he knew he would be feeling every bump in the road in driving the five-and-a-half-hour trip from Beaumont to New Orleans. Mike's secretary set up a flight for Bill and Jan from the Southeast Texas Regional Airport to the airport in New Orleans, car rental, and hotel accommodations. Finally, February 13 arrived. The flight was definitely a blessing over driving. The next morning, Jan drove Bill in their compact red rental car to Dr. Riordan's office.

Dr. Riordan's nurse removed Bill's bandages so none of the doctor's time would be wasted. He was an older doctor with gray hair and a slender frame. He entered Bill's examination room with five younger doctors trailing behind him. These men were not medical students. They were already doctors receiving specialized training regarding hands from the best hand surgeon in the world. He looked at Bill's hand and forearm and asked what had happened. Bill explained the incident as Dr. Riordan looked at the x-rays Bill brought from Dr. Smith's office. Dr. Riordan was short on words and short on tact. He didn't pull any punches. "Well, I can cut your right big toe off and put it on for a thumb," the surgeon explained. "But then, if your body rejects your toe for a thumb, then you've lost a toe and a thumb. I don't know what I'm going to do with you," the doctor continued. "I might be able to do some reconstructive surgery and give you a little bigger thumb. Go back and do some more therapy. Come see me in two months," he said matter-of-factly and handed Bill a script for more therapy. With that, he turned and walked out of the room. The five doctors followed him like puppies following their mama. That was it. The appointment with the greatest hand surgeon in the world was over. He had contact with Bill for a total of four to five minutes. He left with no words of encouragement or words of wisdom.

As Bill and Jan left Dr. Riordan's office, the weather turned bad, and a torrential downpour in New Orleans was expected. As Jan drove the red rental car through the New Orleans traffic, the rage began to build inside Bill until it began to pour out of him. Bill was dumbfounded. He couldn't think straight. He was in shock. He had just visited with a man who was arguably the best hand surgeon in the world. He expected some words of encouragement in those few minutes with Dr. Riordan. Instead, the doctor's words knocked Bill's feet right out from under him and then stomped all over them. He was screaming, crying, and hitting the padded dashboard of the little car with his left fist. "How could Ron be so careless? Why did God let this happen to me? I thought I was supposed to be His child. I thought He was supposed to take care of his children. What kind of a jerk, holier-than-thou stupid doctor was this guy, anyway?" he screamed. He couldn't stop. The anger and rage poured from him for what seemed like forever. He was exploding – just like the nurse warned him about earlier.

Chapter Four

Dusty

"For I, too, was once a son, tenderly loved by my mother as an only child. And the companion of my father."
Proverbs 4:3 – Living Bible

Bill and Jan had been married for over seven years and had not been blessed with children. Some medical problems prevented Jan from carrying a child to full term. God evidently had other plans for their parenthood and led them to the Edna Gladney Home in Fort Worth, Texas. It was advertised as one of the top homes for pregnant teens and adoption centers in the nation. Their application was processed, they were approved, and their wait began. Edna Gladney liked to blend the physical and psychological characteristics of the woman giving birth to the child and the man who got her pregnant, to the potential adoptive parents. Their case worker was a wonderful and caring woman named Zemily Turner. She told them to be patient. The process, she advised, could take a long time. She also told the expectant couple the phone call saying that they were suddenly parents and could come as early as a few weeks, to as long as two years. One thing about adoptions – you never knew how pregnant you were (for lack of a better word). The wait began.

Six months passed and no phone call came from the adoption center. Jan was the impatient one. She would not call Zemily but always talked Bill into calling for them. Zemily's answer to Bill's phone call was always the same. She always said she didn't know anything. She always ended the conversation with, "Just be patient. The call could be today, tomorrow, or months away."

BILL DAVIS

Every two to three months, Jan would pressure Bill about calling Zemily. Her answer was always the same. Zemily would also call Bill, but not in regard to the adoption. Part of the adoption process was to relinquish parental rights by both the woman giving birth to the baby and the man who got her pregnant. Finding the man who got the woman pregnant sometimes became quite a challenge. Zemily called Bill on several occasions when a man needed to be located in Southeast Texas for her civil process. These calls worked out well for both of them. Bill was usually able to provide the information Zemily needed. And, it gave him a chance to ask about their adoption progress without him being the one to initiate the call.

As the months rolled by, Bill stayed busy investigating the child abuse cases that were assigned to him to solve. Lt. Harold Engstrom was now a judge. He was appointed to fill a vacancy in one of the two justice of the peace offices in the county courthouse. Bill was also busy preparing a child abuse seminar that he and his new lieutenant, Weldon Dunlap, decided to present to other police officers and Child Protective Services investigators. Their program was presented on Thursday, July 28, 1983, and it was a big hit. Bill continued to receive phone calls throughout Friday and the following Monday about the seminar and answering questions about presenting the program again.

On Monday, August 1, 1983, Bill was inundated with child abuse cases which required working overtime on many days just to keep up. Many times as he opened a case file to study its contents of physical abuse or sexual molestation of a child and begin the investigation he thought, 'How could someone do this to a child so defenseless and helpless? These people were blessed with one of God's most beautiful miracles – a child – and Jan and I can't have one.'

Freddie Bobb, the secretary for the Special Crimes Bureau, came to Bill's office door late in the day and advised him that his sister, JoAnn, was at the station to visit with him. Freddie would normally have called Bill, but he was already on the telephone talking about an investigation. He was swamped and people were in the lobby waiting to see him. As Bill ended his telephone call, he quickly walked to the lobby and ushered JoAnn into his office. Before he and his sister could begin their visit, Freddie came to Bill's door again and told him another phone call was on hold for him. Bill asked her to take a message, but she quickly advised him that he needed to answer this phone call right away. As usual, he was being pulled in all directions.

Bill's office was located directly behind the lobby of the Special Crimes Bureau. It was the only office where someone could be in the lobby and look directly into an investigator's office. He answered the call that was on hold and it was Zemily. "Long time since I've heard from you," Bill exclaimed being somewhat facetious. Zemily called him earlier that day, asking for help locating a man who had gotten one of the girls at the adoption center pregnant. He helped her with information on the man, and now she was calling again. As swamped as he was, he didn't mind helping her. However, Bill's impatience and being on overload obviously showed. He hadn't even had time to sit down as he answered Zemily's call.

"How's it going?" Zemily inquired. "Swamped, as usual," Bill replied. He slowed himself down and was very cordial to his case worker. "I need to ask you a question," Zemily continued. "Sure, who do we need to locate?" Bill replied, obviously sure he knew the nature of her call. "I need to know if you would like to be the father of a six-day-old, six-pound, six-ounce little boy?" she asked in a very calm voice. Bill hesitated, he couldn't talk for several seconds. When he did speak, his voice was trembling. "Zemily, that's not funny! Don't be kidding me like this," Bill said. "I'm not kidding," Zemily replied. "You're a daddy!" It was 4:30 p.m.

Bill had never fainted in his life. But in that moment, his legs turned to jelly. He had to flop down in the chair behind his desk. His voice got louder, "Zemily, don't be joking with me!" he shouted. Suddenly, everyone in the immediate area knew something was going on. Freddie ran to Bill's office door. JoAnn jumped up from her chair as she heard her brother's loud tone. Tears started streaming down Bill's face. Something had to be terribly wrong. The two ladies could not imagine what had happened to cause Bill to suddenly be crying. He had a yellow legal pad on his desk. As he continued talking to Zemily he wrote on the pad, 'I'M A DAD! IT'S A BOY!'

Somehow, Bill managed to think somewhat clearly. "Why did you call me instead of Jan?" Bill asked. Zemily laughed on her end of the phone and said, "For eighteen months Jan always asked you to call instead of calling herself. So, I thought since you were always the one to call and inquire, you should be the first one to get the phone call."

Through all the commotion, Bill managed to hear Zemily ask him when he and Jan could come to get their baby. It was late in the day. It was too late to be there the next day. Preparations needed to be made. They were going to get their son. "Wednesday morning, at 10:00 a.m.!" Bill declared. Zemily made the notation on her calendar and ended the conversation with "We'll see you then, Dad."

People came from everywhere throughout the station. Even witnesses that were in the lobby to see other detectives were congratulating Bill. He needed to get in touch with Jan. She had already gotten off from work at the sheriff's department. She was sick with a sinus infection and went to Dr. Fama's office after work. Bill quickly called their office. The receptionist informed Bill that Jan was there and Dr. Fama had just gone into the examination room with her. "Interrupt them," Bill said. "This is an emergency." The seconds passed and Jan's voice came on the line. "Hey, what's wrong?" she asked. "Nothing's wrong, Mom," Bill said. "Do what?" she yelled. "I just thought you would want to know that Zemily called. You are now the mother of a six-day-old little boy. We have our son, Dusty!" Bill proclaimed. All he could hear was screaming on the phone. "I'll see you at home!" she yelled and the phone went dead.

Bill couldn't drive fast enough from Beaumont to Dallas. He and Jan stayed that night with her brother, Larry, and his family.

LOOK OUT SATAN ~ GOD'S AT WORK!

Wednesday was a day that would change both Jan's and Bill's lives forever. They drove to the Edna Gladney Home in Fort Worth. Their sister-in-law, Jan (yep, two Jans in the same car), accompanied them on the momentous journey. It was one thing to be pregnant and slowly prepare for the journey to the hospital. It was quite another thing to not be parents one day and suddenly have a baby the next day. The feelings were scary but exciting. As they arrived in the Edna Gladney parking lot, they knew they would be leaving with a very special passenger on board.

Bill carried the empty infant carrier into the waiting area as he and the two Jans informed the receptionist they were there to see Zemily. The caseworker entered the lobby and escorted the three to a special room. She left again and returned a short time later with a little bundle in her arms. Jan held her son first. A few minutes later, it was Bill's turn. As he held his son, he was very careful, almost as if the tiny package would break. Dusty evidently sensed Bill's uneasiness and began to whimper. He began to talk softly to his son and rock him in his arms. Everything was going to be okay.

Bill handed Dusty over to Jan. There was a mountain of paperwork to sign. Once the paperwork was completed, they were free to go. Zemily advised them she would make a home visit in the next two to four months and would let them know of the date. They were now the temporary parents of a beautiful baby boy. A court hearing would take place in about six months, and a Tarrant County Family Court district judge would finalize the adoption.

Bill handed out "It's A Boy" cigars at work and Jan took a maternity leave of six weeks from the sheriff's department. The days, weeks, and months seemed to fly by. Zemily came about three months into their parenthood and conducted her home visit. She could tell that this child was in a loving home, and she would include these positive comments in her report to the judge.

Finally, the telephone call came from Zemily. It was time to go before the judge and make Dusty their child, permanently. It was the first week in February 1984.

The trip from Beaumont to Dallas was uneventful. Bill rode in the backseat of their van with Dusty while Jan drove. Zemily did not tell Bill and Jan to bring Dusty to the adoption hearing. They did not know that family court judges consider adoption day in their courts a very festive occasion. Sister-in-law Jan babysat Dusty while Bill and Jan made the forty-five-mile trip to the Tarrant County Courthouse. They entered the courthouse and found Zemily. The first thing she noticed was Bill's bandages and the sling around his neck supporting his arm and hand. Of course, her immediate response was, "What happened?" Bill told her of the hunting accident.

She was quite shaken and escorted them into a room where the three could have some privacy. "You should have informed me of this accident," she told the couple. "It's okay," Bill explained. He told her that he would be seeing a doctor next week that was considered the greatest hand specialist in the world. "No, it's not okay," Zemily explained. "I know that accidents happen," she replied. "But, you must realize if you were killed, I would have had to take Dusty away from Jan if this adoption was not finalized." Obviously in shock over what they had just been told, the couple barely heard Zemily say that Edna Gladney wanted their babies to go to a home with both a father and a mother. If Bill had been killed in the hunting accident, Dusty would have been taken from Jan and placed with another couple. Zemily and the Edna Gladney Home were adamant that Dusty should start his life with a two-parent family.

"Well, you're alive and mending," Zemily said, clearing the air in the tiny room. "Let's make you Dusty's permanent parents." God's protection exhibited itself once again.

Bill and Jan entered the courtroom and it was like a circus. Bill had been in lots of courtrooms in his career. They were always quiet and orderly. This courtroom was totally different. The bailiff announced the Judge as the man in the black robe entered the courtroom. He was smiling as he called the first parents' names. He had them raise their right hands, swore them in, and then asked the couple a series of questions. When he finished, the Judge came down from his bench and stood with the couple and their new baby as relatives and friends took pictures. The Judge continued this process until Jan's and Bill's names were called. The couple approached the bench. The Judge obviously noticed Bill's hand and arm bandaged and his arm in a sling. "What happened?" the Judge asked. Bill told him the story of the hunting accident.

After Bill finished his summary, the Judge asked the whereabouts of Dusty. Jan told the Judge that they were not advised it was okay to bring him. She explained that she and Bill were both in law enforcement and knew courtrooms were supposed to be quiet and orderly and was afraid Dusty would start crying and be disruptive. With that explanation, the Judge proceeded with the court hearing on Dusty. He told them to raise their right hands and be sworn in. As Bill tried to remove his arm from the sling, the Judge laughed and said, "Never mind your right hand, Mr. Davis. Your left hand will do just fine." The Judge chuckled again and said, "I don't think I've ever had someone raise their left hand in my courtroom before." With that, he swore them in. He asked Bill and Jan the standard questions about taking care of Dusty and providing him with a good and loving home. With the questions all done, he declared Dustin Carl Davis to be the son of Janice Louise Rawlinson Davis and Billy Frank Davis. He was now their son – FOREVER!

Dusty's First Baby Pictures

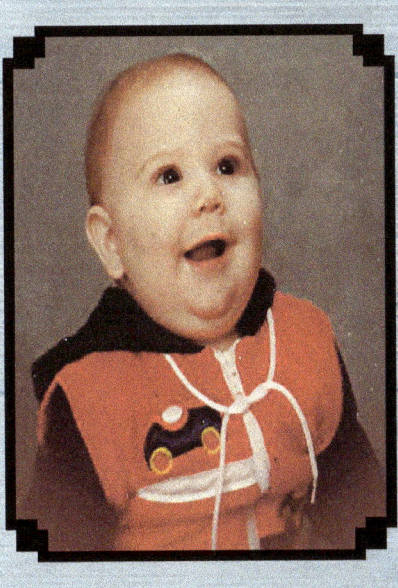

Chapter Five

Back to Work

"I can do all things through Christ who strengthens me."
Philippians 4:13 - NKJV

The weeks went by and Bill went to therapy five days a week for the first two weeks. The sessions then dropped to three days a week. Bill tried to do the exercises that Penny gently pushed him to do, but it seemed that no progress was being made. Depression slowly started setting in on Bill. Was he going to have to live the rest of his life with one hand? The police department was being very patient. Bill had weeks and weeks of sick leave built up, but he knew he would have to return to work at some point or lose his job. A stack of cases was on his desk needing to be investigated. How would he type affidavits and other items of paperwork that were required of him to conduct investigations?

It was finally time. Bill awoke early. He had been off work for eight weeks. The time went by slowly, and yet very quickly. After a few minor cuts, he learned to shave with his left hand. He could shower without his bandages. He still put the pieces of silicone and his wrist brace in place and wrapped the ace bandage from his hand to his elbow. He put his finger splints in place. He eased his pistol into the left waistband of his slacks. He was ready to go. (The purpose of the finger splints was to put pressure on Bill's fingers and straighten them out. The pain caused by the splints was so intense, he could only stand them for a short period of time. His goal was to put the finger splints on several times a day, until one day his fingers would be straight again. This process would take over six months to straighten his fingers.)

BILL DAVIS

Everyone was glad to see him back in his office. Lt. Dunlap greeted him and assured him everything was going to be okay. He settled in and picked up one of the case folders on his desk. It was time to get back to work. Children needed to be saved.

Phone calls were made and appointments were set. A lot of paperwork and a lot of typing is required when investigating crimes that television shows never depict. Bill's first appointment arrived. He and his witness muddled through Bill's typing with one hand. This process was interesting, especially typing on an electric typewriter, not a computer.

Bill's therapy appointment was usually after lunch. This schedule made the day more efficient. He left for lunch, went to therapy, and then returned to his office to work and finish the day.

The wounds were slowly healing. Penny debrided Bill's thumb and forearm every therapy session. She worked diligently on getting mobility back into his fingers, hand, wrist, and forearm. Penny warned Bill about reaching into cabinets and drawers. She explained that he could easily get cut and not feel the injury if he did not look into drawers every time he reached for something. The injured nerves would not allow him to feel something sharp for a long time, and he could easily be re-injured during his rehabilitation process. She gave him a special spoon, knife, and fork to use at every meal. The utensils had large round pieces of foam rubber that ran the length of the handles and were about two inches thick. She encouraged Bill to use his right hand more and more instead of using his left hand for everything.

The feeling in Bill's hand and wrist were a mixture of sensations. His forearm, hand, index, middle finger, and nub were numb, yet hurt all the time. His ring and little finger felt okay. Bill asked about this on one of his visits with Dr. Smith. The doctor explained that two main nerves go to the fingers. One nerve branches out and goes to the thumb, index, and middle digits. The second nerve goes to the ring and little finger. He further explained that the shotgun blast damaged the nerve to the thumb, index, and middle finger. Bill's question was, "Will I get the feeling back?" The doctor explained that nerves grow very slowly, but the feeling should return. He told Bill to be patient. It may take up to a year for the feeling to return.

Therapy was like a roller coaster. One day would be good. Everything Bill and Penny did in therapy that day seemed to work and they made great strides. On those days, Bill would return to work on a positive note. Sometimes on the next session, it seemed like nothing was being accomplished. Sometimes it felt as though therapy was going backward. On these days, Bill would return to work after therapy in a total state of depression. He always called his friend and SWAT team colleague, Lt. Pat O'Quinn. Pat was a Vietnam veteran and was seriously wounded in the war when a fellow soldier stepped on a land mine. Pat received shrapnel in both legs. Pat told Bill that at one point when he was in the hospital, his depression got so bad that he would have thrown himself out of his third-story hospital room window and ended it all. But, he couldn't get out of his hospital bed to get to the window. On these occasions when therapy wasn't going well, Pat would enter Bill's office and close the door. Bill poured his heart out to his friend, telling him how bad therapy had gone, how nothing was working, and how nothing was progressing. His friend listened. His friend had been there. It was okay to cry. It was okay to be angry. It was okay to be depressed. Pat's visits helped Bill more than Pat probably realized. Penny helped with the physical therapy. Pat helped with the emotional therapy. A psychologist or therapist could read about helping problems like this in a book. But, they had not been there. Pat had, and it made a huge difference.

Some things were quite difficult, and now looking back, were quite funny. Bill wore his slacks, boots, and dress shirt every day to work as he had always done since becoming a detective. One day, in particular, became one of those days Bill would never forget. Jan began work at 7:00 a.m. and Bill began work at 8:00 a.m. Since returning to work, Bill would get up earlier than usual so Jan could help him get dressed. Bill showered with a plastic bag over his bandaged arm to keep the bandages dry. When getting dressed, Jan helped Bill tuck his shirt into his slacks and hooked the clasp of the waistband. Shortly after Bill arrived for work, he got the urge to go to the bathroom, which was no big deal as this was his regular routine every day.

However, this was the first time that he'd worn this particular pair of slacks since the accident. He entered the restroom and entered a vacant stall. He easily unbuckled his belt and the waistband clasp of his pants with one hand. With business taken care of, he exited the stall but had not yet hooked and zipped his pants. Bill had learned by standing in front of a mirror to pull his pants up higher than normal and hold them in place with his right elbow. Then watching in the mirror, he would take his left hand and pull the waistband to the right until he could hook it and then zip the fly with his left hand. This day would be a little different. He couldn't get the two sides of the hook on his waistband, hooked. He tried and tried. He watched in the restroom mirror as the two sides of the clasp would come within a fraction of an inch to each other, but refused to hook one into the other. Sweat began pouring down his face. He couldn't get his pants fixed. He couldn't just walk out of the restroom with his pants undone. The situation became comical, yet desperate. What was he going to do? He thought about sneaking back to his office but then he thought, 'what if he lost the grip on the waistband with his right elbow?' Then, he would be standing with his slacks all the way to the floor. He nixed that idea. He was leaning against the lavatory, catching his breath and trying to come up with another bright idea when one of his detective friends entered the restroom. The detective could see the sweat pouring down Bill's face and dripping off his chin. He knew something was wrong. "I can't get my pants hooked and zipped," Bill exclaimed. His detective friend knew of Bill's accident and surveyed the situation. He realized he couldn't take care of his own business in the restroom and then just walk out. He had to help.

LOOK OUT SATAN ~ GOD'S AT WORK!

He looked around the restroom and saw that no one else was present. He quickly hooked Bill's pants and zipped them for him. "If you ever tell a soul about this, I'll kill you," his friend declared. Bill thanked him and promised his lips were sealed.

(They still are!)

SWAT training was definitely different. Captain Joe Crutchfield, commander of the SWAT team, and Lt. Bruce Thomason, assistant commander of the SWAT team, kept Bill on the team, allowing him time to heal. One of the great assets of the SWAT team was that they practiced shooting their pistols with both hands. This practice helped Bill switch to wearing his pistol from the right side to the left side. SWAT team training was usually fun but always physical and strenuous. These guys were trained and prepared for anything. Everyone practiced various roles on the team. One moment the practice session might have one guy being number one through a door on a hard-entry team. The next moment, that same person might be the team's rear guard. Everyone had to be familiar with various roles and be proficient with that role if called upon to perform that task at a moment's notice.

There was one role that everyone did not practice. It was the position of the sniper. The team had three snipers, and Bill was one of them. At most training sessions, the snipers practiced by themselves for a few hours, honing their marksmanship skills. About three months after returning to work, Bill decided it was time to pull out his rifle. His brain was trained to have hand-eye coordination with his right eye and his right index finger. His rifle was a Steyr-Mannlicher .308 caliber bolt action rifle with a ten-power competition scope mounted on it. Its trigger system had double triggers. The rifle could be fired with a normal front trigger pull. Or, the rear set trigger could be pulled, leaving the front trigger with a pull that could be set to be more or less sensitive. Bill had the set-trigger to be extremely sensitive with only a couple of pounds of pull. Bill's right index finger was accustomed to the trigger setting. His left index finger was not. He pulled the butt of the rifle snugly into his left shoulder. Doug York, one of the other snipers, watched Bill's target one-hundred yards away through a spotting scope. Bill slowly pulled the rear set trigger. His left index finger slowly touched the front trigger. The jolt was sudden and unexpected as the rifle fired. "Uh, the target's still clean," Doug reported. Bill suddenly realized just how sensitive his rifle's trigger really was. It would take several more rounds and a sore shoulder, but he came to be proficient with his rifle shooting left-handed as he had formerly been right-handed.

"Are you going to go to lunch?" Sgt. Denny Starks asked Bill as they passed each other in the atrium of the police station's second floor. It was 11:30 a.m. "Shortly," Bill replied. Bill took a few more steps, and then turned to inquire about lunch from his friend. Denny was a detective in the fraud division. Bill was a child abuse and sex crimes detective. Denny had been a member of the police department of what seemed like forever. Bill had been on the police department for almost twelve years. In that time, he and Denny had never gone to lunch together. They were working colleagues but they worked in two separate divisions. Except for being in the detective division, they had nothing in common. "Why did you ask?" Bill inquired of his friend. "So we could get a close parking place (handicapped parking)," his friend declared. Denny laughed as he opened the door to the detective division. Bill couldn't help but shake his head and laugh. Moments like this meant a lot to Bill. These moments helped him conquer his fight with depression. His friends were compassionate but they never let him feel sorry for himself. They were true friends.

Therapy continued with Penny. Bill returned to New Orleans for his second visit with Dr. Riordan. The doctor was impressed with Bill's mobility and strength in his arm and hand. He prescribed four more months of therapy and stated that Bill's hand and arm should be strong enough by August for reconstructive surgery. Finally, Bill received some encouraging words from the world's greatest hand surgeon.

In August 1984, Bill received a great birthday present. It was

LOOK OUT SATAN ~ GOD'S AT WORK!

a present he would cherish for the rest of his life – reconstructive surgery on his amputated thumb. Dr. Riordan moved some muscles and ligaments around which gave Bill a slightly larger nub with greater dexterity. Therapy with Penny continued for the rest of the year. In 1985, Bill slowly switched his pistol from his left side, back to his right side. Sensation in his fingers slowly came back. He was able to switch from shooting his sniper rifle from his left shoulder and left finger, back to his right side. Life was getting back to normal. There was one exception. When children wanted a 'High 5' from Officer Bill, they got a 'High 4.'

Members of the Beaumont Police S.W.A.T. Team are practicing Defensive Tactics.

The Beaumont Police S.W.A.T. Team practicing repelling at the Beaumont Fire Department's Training Facility. Bill is repelling from the 6th floor of the training tower.

Beaumont Police S.W.A.T. Team members in the latter 1970s. Kneeling (L-R): Robert Compton, Jim Singletary, Pat O'Quinn, Gene Roberts, S.W.A.T. Commander Captain Joe Crutchfield. Standing (L-R): Chuck Ashworth, Sonny Chambers, Bruce Thomason, Robert Roberts, Bill Davis.

Chapter Six

God's Preparations

"For we are God's handiwork, recreated in Christ Jesus, that we may do those good works which God predestined for us, that we should walk in them." Ephesians 2:10 – Amplified Bible

Being in front of an audience never bothered Bill. In fact, he enjoyed it. His mom always took him and his sister, JoAnn, to church. She made sure they had a Christian upbringing. Bill also loved to sing. Bill's career of standing in front of an audience began as young as his junior high school years. Brother Clyde Jones was the music director at their Baptist church in Groves, Texas. He asked Bill to sing special music for the Sunday morning church service on a regular basis. Sometimes, Bro. Clyde's son, Bill, joined Bill in singing. The two Bills made a great duet. As the years passed, Bro. Clyde moved on and his son, George, became the music director. Then when George moved away from the area, Bill was asked to be the music director for the church. It was a great honor for someone who was only a high school student to be the music director for his church. He continued this job until he left for college.

Bill's best friend, Paul Martin, came forward during church one Sunday and advised Brother James Stroud, the church pastor, that he felt the Lord had called him to preach. Bill and Paul made a fine youth team. Many local churches asked this duo to sing and preach on special occasions. Then in 1967, Bill's junior year in high school, he felt the Lord tugging at his own heart to preach as well as sing. Bill preached ninety-nine youth sermons and revivals from his junior year until he graduated from high school.

One school day during the spring of 1968, Bill's high school counselor summoned him to her office. A college recruiter was there from a small Christian college in East Texas. Dr. Eugene Moore, Director of Admissions for East Texas Baptist College, was making a recruiting visit to several high schools and one of the schools on his list was Port Neches-Groves High School. Ms. Smith introduced Dr. Moore to Bill and explained that Bill was a Christian and felt God had called him into the ministry. Dr. Moore spent time with Bill, showing him a pamphlet about the college and explaining that he felt that ETBC was the place for Bill. Many young ministers attended the college and he felt that Bill would fit right in with their program.

A family friend, Mr. Fletcher Garner, was loyal to Stephen F. Austin State University in Nacogdoches and tried to persuade Bill to consider his alma mater. Paul attended Jacksonville Baptist College in Jacksonville, Texas. SFA seemed too big to Bill and JBC was too small. JBC was also only a two-year school, and Bill wanted to attend a college with a four-year plan. ETBC seemed just right. It wasn't too big or too small, and it was also a four-year college. A visit to the ETBC campus a few weeks later confirmed that this was the college for him. It was a beautiful campus located on the highest hill in Marshall, Texas. The campus chapel sat on the highest point of the hill and it could be seen for miles. Bill planned his fall courses with one of the school's advisors. Interestingly, he did not begin his college career majoring in Theology, as all the young ministers on campus did. He planned his curriculum to major in Business Administration.

Bill's dad, Carl F. Davis, died March 1, 1967, during Bill's junior year at PNG. His dad was only fifty-six years old. The death of Bill's dad also placed a lot of pressure on him. He was the only son and the eldest child. He was also the only male child on his father's side to carry on the family name. His dad's death forced him to step up to an adult role much faster than many of his high school classmates. It also forced him to miss out on participating in some school functions that his classmates enjoyed during his senior year in high school, such as the school prom.

It was September 1968. He was transitioning from high school to college life. It was tough for Bill to leave his mom, Nevada, and JoAnn, who was four years younger than him. However, beginning college was exciting. It was the start of a new chapter in Bill's life.

Bill spent his first college semester living in Feagin Hall. His roommate was a young man from Guatemala City, Guatemala, named Carlos Lee. Somehow, Bill fell into the companionship of a college junior named Chip Smith from Bridge City, Texas. Maybe it was the geographical closeness of Groves, Texas, and Bridge City, Texas. Chip was not one of the college ministerial students. He wore cowboy boots and jeans. On one of their excursions out of class, Chip took Bill to 'THE' western store in Marshall, Texas. Long's Western Store on Hwy. 59 South was owned by a wonderful couple, Johnny and Pat Long. Before long, Bill was making the trip to Long's Western Store several times a week. He enjoyed the smell of leather as he entered the store, and he enjoyed the company of Johnny and Pat Long.

Chip introduced Bill to another college junior, Richard Shirey. Richard lived about seventy-five miles away in Jacksonville, Texas, and he would go home to visit his parents, J.B. and Mae Shirey, every weekend. Before long, Chip and Richard were bringing their freshman friend along on Friday afternoons for a weekend trek to Jacksonville. The weekends were always fun at the Shirey's. J.B., a decorated Korean War veteran, always had horses and it wasn't long before Bill was riding horses and trying his hand at roping. A few months later, J.B. sold Bill his first horse, a blue roan named Buddy, and let Bill pay for him over time. He was turning into a cowboy.

Bill only had a few hundred dollars in savings to begin his college career, and that money only lasted a few weeks. Bill received a social security check and a veteran's check every month because of his dad's death. However, he rarely saw a penny from those checks because his mom needed the money to pay the house note and other bills in Groves. Bill's weekend trips to Jacksonville were fun, but he needed to work. J.B. helped Bill secure a job at a plastics factory in Jacksonville, working the day shift on Saturdays and Sundays. One

LOOK OUT SATAN ~ GOD'S AT WORK!

of the main plastic items made for many years at the factory was a round Army green colored plastic collar that was part of a specific bomb that was being used at that time in the Vietnam war. The job helped Bill with extra spending money for gas, horse feed, and hay. As the spring semester of Bill's freshman year was ending, the plastics factory hit a slump and Bill was laid off. He needed a job, and again, J.B. came to the rescue. He introduced Bill to Mr. Ed Moore, a man in his seventies who seemed to always have some money-making idea going. His latest endeavor was snow cones. Mr. Moore invested in a cargo truck and an ice-making machine. Bill had the 'coolest' job in town, driving around all day with music blasting through the truck's loudspeaker letting everyone know the snow cone man was near.

Bill didn't want to impose on the Shirey's hospitality that summer. So, he rented a room at a local boarding house. Jacksonville was known for having some of the best watermelons in the southern United States. Bill stopped by the local farmer's market every morning and bought a small watermelon. He put it at the bottom of his ice bin and then loaded the bin with ice for the day's snow cones. It was a real treat at the end of almost every day to enjoy the taste of one of the world's best cold watermelons, right out of the fields of East Texas.

Mr. Moore had a big sorrel-colored horse with a white-blazed face, named Big John. The gelding was part Tennessee walker and part Morgan. Both breeds were big, and Big John was a really big horse. Bill and Mr. Moore agreed to a trade. Mr. Moore took Buddy and Bill took the big sorrel. The horse was so big that when Bill saddled him, the saddle horn was over six feet in the air. It took a while, but Bill practiced and was able to hold onto the saddle horn and swing himself onto Big John's back without using the stirrup. It was a cool and impressive move. Big John was one of the smoothest horses Bill ever rode. The big sorrel could be at a dead run and it was like rocking in a rocking chair.

Bill was now a sophomore at ETBC. He continued his visits

one or two times a week to Long's Western Store. He seldom bought anything, he just enjoyed the visit. Johnny and Pat had a beautiful two-hundred-acre ranch outside Marshall with several heads of black Angus cows, a couple of horses, and a poodle named Brandy. Johnny had some cattle pens built out of one-inch pipes next to his barn. The used pipes were rusty. He hired Richard, Chip, and Bill to scrape all of the pipes with wire brushes and then paint them with aluminum paint. It was a tedious and boring task. But for Bill, it was a job.

Johnny made several unexpected trips from the store to the ranch while the young men were working on the corral. The task of scraping and painting pipes for what seemed like miles and miles was finally finished. It was getting close to Thanksgiving and Johnny needed extra help in the store. The one young man that Johnny came to depend on was Bill. On one of his unexpected trips to the ranch, Johnny offered Bill a job as a salesman in the store. Johnny told him the job may only last through the Christmas holidays. It didn't matter. Bill was elated. He was going to get to go to work at his most favorite store in the entire town, smelling the sweet smell of leather every time he entered the door.

Bill attended his classes and then went to work at the store. Christmastime at Long's Western Store was crazy. The store was always packed with folks wanting boots, jeans, cowboy hats, and other western wear. Finally, it was Christmas Eve. Bill drove home for Christmas with his mom and JoAnn. On Christmas Day afternoon, however, Bill left and returned to Marshall. Johnny needed his new employee to help with the rush the day after Christmas. The store was packed.

The job continued past Christmas and into January. Bill was turning out to be a good employee. Many of the store's patrons came in and saw the young man. They asked Pat if the young man was her son. Johnny and Pat had no children, but Pat just said, "Yep, that's our boy." Before long, Bill was calling the two, "Mama and Johnny." They even laughed and told some folks that Bill was a stray they had taken in. Johnny loved to hunt. But, the duties of the store prohibited him from getting to relax and enjoy this past-time as often as he wanted to. He was raised in Winnfield, Louisiana, and Huey P. Long and John Long were his uncles. Now that Bill was a male presence in the store, Johnny decided to take his brother, Clifford, up on an end-of-the-season hunt on the last weekend of deer season after the holidays. While he was gone, Bill worked diligently in the store with Mama and, Toy, a lady that had worked for Mama and Johnny for a number of years.

One morning Bill had just swept off the front porch of the store and walked back inside when a man entered the western store. One look at this man and it was easy to see that he was in a foul mood. Someone purchased a hat for him as a Christmas present and he was not happy with the style of the crease that was in the hat. Mama did everything she could to please the man but his foul demeanor got even worse. Bill stood quietly behind Pat. It was her store and she was diligently attempting to please this customer. Suddenly, the man threw the hat on the floor, almost hitting Pat with it, and started cursing. He wasn't just cursing to yell some profane words. He was aiming those words at Pat. This man was now cursing Bill's new 'mama.' That was it. Bill came from behind Pat and started after the man. His fists were clenched. Bill told the man, in no uncertain terms, to leave or he would throw him out the door or through the door – it didn't matter which. "You're not talking to my mama like that and get away with it!" Bill yelled in a very loud voice. The man evidently didn't want to tangle with the wiry nineteen-year-old and ran out the door. Both Bill's dad and Johnny taught him to be respectful of women and to protect them. The man never returned. Johnny returned from the deer hunt and Pat told him about the hat incident. Bill was nearby and was listening to the story. As Pat finished, Johnny looked at Bill. "Boy, you did good. And don't worry, if you would have hit him and gone to jail, I would have bonded you out!" he said with a grin.

In January, Johnny, Pat, and Bill traveled to Dallas after closing the store one Saturday evening. They attended an annual market show where Johnny ordered thousands of dollars in merchandise for the store. They returned to Marshall on Sunday evening and took Bill to his dorm. Johnny and Pat could not believe how loud the noise was as they neared the building. It was the end of the Christmas break and classes were to resume the next morning. "How can you study?" Johnny asked Bill, referring to the noise coming from inside the dormitory. "It's not easy," Bill replied. A week later, Johnny asked Bill if he would like to come and live at the ranch with them. Bill could not believe his ears. He moved most of his clothes from his dorm room into his room at their home the next day. It was a place Bill would call home for over a year. A short time later Pat and Johnny were affectionately called "Mama and Pappy." They had become his surrogate parents.

As Bill's college years went by, he occasionally thought about how he was not preaching. He wondered if the 'preaching' idea had been a mistake. His goal in life now was to own his own western store. So, he continued majoring in Business instead of Theology. Bill didn't know why, but his minor in English slowly evolved. It wasn't something he planned. His writing and grammatical abilities increased. One of his favorite classes was Speech-131. Standing in front of people and speaking seemed so easy and natural to him. Visiting and waiting on people every day at Long's Western Store came naturally. It seemed that he never met a stranger.

In January 1971, Bill left Marshall and returned home. Yep, it was because of a girl. He and Charlene dated in high school. But once he started college, the distance caused the romance not to last. Then one day during his junior year in college, out of the blue he received a letter from her and the romance was on once again. He had to be closer to her.

In moving back home, Bill had to tell Mama and Pappy he was leaving. They had an idea the move might be coming. Bill began going home to Groves almost every Saturday night after the store closed to see Charlene. He would return to Marshall early the

LOOK OUT SATAN ~ GOD'S AT WORK!

following Monday morning to help Pappy open the store before going to classes. Bill deeply loved Mama and Pappy and telling them he was leaving was one of the hardest things he would ever do. Their relationship was strong and it would last for many years.

Bill attended the spring semester at Lamar University in Beaumont, Texas, and went to work for a local health spa as a weightlifting instructor. He enjoyed the job because he had been pumping iron since he was sixteen years old. He was able to work out and stay in shape while working at the facility, but the money was not that great. A few months later, he changed occupations and went to work for a local finance company. The job was okay, but it still wasn't what he wanted. A friend from Bill's pre-college days, Phillip Galloway, was listening to Bill describe how he wanted something different. "Come work for Port Arthur P.D.," Phillip said. Bill never thought of being a police officer. Phillip made the job sound quite exciting.

The Port Arthur Police Department posted their police officer entrance examination. It was to be given the last week in July 1971. About ten people showed up for the test. As Bill approached the city employee administering the exam to receive his copy of the test, the man told Bill, "You're not yet twenty-one years old. You can't take the test." Bill retorted and said, "You're not hiring anyone in the next two weeks. I'll be twenty-one when you're ready to hire me." The man looked at Bill, smiled, and handed him a test. Bill thanked the man and took a seat to begin the entrance exam. 'Where did that reply come from?' Bill thought as he began his test. Once again, that quiet, small voice gave Bill the words to say.

Two officers were hired by the Port Arthur Police Department on August 25, 1971 – Gene Christian and Bill Davis. Both of the men began a career on that day that would last a lifetime for each of them.

A riot occurred on New Year's Eve night, in 1971. Some of the brass in the P.A.P.D. wanted to blame the incident on one of the black midnight shift officers. A couple of inspectors cornered Bill as he was getting off his midnight shift and tried to pressure him into lying for them so they could get rid of the officer in question. "I'm running fever and sick with the flu, but I worked my shift last night," Bill told the high-ranking officers. "I'm not going to lie for you, and I'm not going to lie for him," Bill declared. "He (the officer in question) did not hit his prisoner while in handcuffs," Bill stated. "If you like your job, you need to tell us what we want to know," one of the inspectors declared sarcastically. "If that's not good enough for you, then take my badge," Bill said. He was honest. It was a trait instilled in him by his parents. The inspectors realized this young officer was not going to bend for them or anyone else. He was dismissed and went home. Bill turned in his resignation, effective two weeks later. He was not going to tolerate lying or any type of corruption. Bill's two 'dads,' his father and Johnny Long, both taught him that a man's word was his bond, and a man's handshake was his seal to a contract.

Bill started working part-time for a local western store during the Christmas holidays of 1971 as a second job. After leaving the Port Arthur Police Department, he worked full-time for the western store throughout the first half of 1972. However, the excitement of law enforcement kept calling him. He filled out an application to be hired by the Beaumont Police Department in the spring of 1972. He and Charlene had also set a date at the end of May to be married. One week before the wedding, Bill was laid off at the western store. He was completely distraught. The invitations had already been mailed. All the arrangements had been finalized. Charlene's uncle, Harold Broussard, who owned a concrete business, told the couple to go ahead with their wedding. He would see that Bill had a job until the police department called him. The wedding went through with no problems. He and Charlene took a short weekend honeymoon and then returned home. Bill was twenty-one years old and in great physical shape – or so he thought. Uncle Harold put Bill behind the handles of a wheelbarrow full of concrete, and a shovel and taught him about 'real' work. Bill's concrete career lasted about two weeks. It was a two-week career he would never forget. Thank God, the

LOOK OUT SATAN ~ GOD'S AT WORK!

Beaumont Police Department called and wanted him to go to work. Bill's experience with Port Arthur P.D. helped him and he was hired as a patrol officer with Beaumont P.D. in June 1972. One week later Bill came home from work. He could tell something was not right with Charlene. "I'm not happy being married. I want to go home," she said. Her suitcase was packed. They had dated off and on for about three years. Their marriage lasted three weeks.

Trying to continue his law enforcement career with Beaumont P.D. while going through a divorce took a great toll on Bill. He needed someone to talk to. His mother was quite difficult to talk to, so he drove to Marshall on one of his days off. He could talk to Mama and Pappy about anything. Bill updated them on everything going on. "Come on back up here. I'll let you be assistant manager and you can slowly buy me out," Johnny said. Bill couldn't believe his ears. At one time, one of his goals was to own his own western store. And now, an established western store was being laid in his lap. He returned to Beaumont and turned in his resignation to the police department, effective October 17, 1972.

Bill's mother hated to see him leave Southeast Texas for a second time. But, Bill enjoyed the smell of leather as he arrived for work every day. Mama and Pappy found a cute rental house for Bill to live in as he returned to their store. The divorce was finalized the week before Bill returned to Marshall. He felt he was turning the page to a new chapter in his life.

A lot of law enforcement officers did business with Long's Western Store. They bought a lot of their equipment, especially boots, and hats from the store. Bill was reminded of his short-lived law enforcement career every time a city officer, county deputy, or Department of Public Safety trooper entered the store. Sometimes the officers came in just to visit with Johnny and relax for a few minutes.

Bill never forgot the first time Texas Ranger Glenn Elliott entered the store. Ranger Elliott was the first Texas Ranger Bill had ever seen. He was over six feet tall and had graying hair and steel-blue eyes. He wore his Texas Ranger badge on a western-styled shirt and packed a .45 caliber semi-automatic pistol on a custom-made Ranger belt. Ranger Elliott bought his western hats from Johnny, and Johnny always made sure to have the hat's creases perfect for him. To say Ranger Elliott was impressive was an understatement. (Ranger Elliott's book, <u>Glenn Elliott – A Ranger's Ranger</u>, was published in 1999. Bill's book, <u>So Innocent, Yet So Dead</u>, was published in December 1998. The two law enforcement officers/authors exchanged books in 2005.)

Finally, the calling was too great. Bill couldn't put his finger on it, but he knew God was drawing him back into a career in law enforcement for some reason. Bill placed a call to Captain Eugene "Seaport" Corder the first week in December. It had only been six weeks, but Bill knew his career in life was destined to be a cop. "It'll take a few weeks to take care of the paperwork," Capt. Corder advised, "but we'll be glad to have you back here." Once again, Bill dreaded telling Mama and Pappy of his decision. He loved them dearly. He knew he was giving up a career that could easily make him financially wealthy in only a few years. But, that still, quiet voice was talking to him, telling him there were lots of ways to be rich besides monetarily. Mama and Pappy understood. Bill was sworn back in as a Beaumont police officer on February 17, 1973.

A few months passed and Bill was in his element. He was on day-shift patrol with many of the same officers he worked with a few months earlier. Within two weeks, Bill was back in the groove and riding as a senior officer in the car with a partner. Captain C.W. Kelly, Bill's commanding officer on the second watch, the day shift, was as cranky and grouchy as he was during Bill's first tenure with Beaumont P.D. Capt. Kelly was from the 'old school.' Chief Bauer liked to see officers wearing a police cap, also a style from the 'old school,' but patrol officers hated them. Capt. Kelly liked the cap and hardly anyone ever saw his black wavy hair under his police cap. His uniform was always pressed and spotless. His boots were always shined.

One day an officer made the mistake of asking if the Captain's weapon, a semi-automatic nickel-plated pistol with silver inlaid grips, was a .45. Capt. Kelly stared at the officer and began a tirade, "I wouldn't be caught dead with a .45. It's a .38 Super and don't you ever forget it. I carry a real gun, not a trotline weight!" No one in the vicinity hearing the conversation ever forgot the caliber of the Captain's gun.

Senior officers loved to bring their rookie officers with their first report to be analyzed by Capt. Kelly. The rookie was, of course, nervous about taking their first report to the 'ol man.' The senior officer helped the rookie word the report correctly, so the rookie figured there would not be a problem. Bringing that first report to the Captain was a part of their initiation. The senior officer always knew to stand a few feet behind the rookie as he handed his report over to the Captain for approval. The rookie stood in front of the 'ol man's' desk waiting for his initials of approval on their paperwork. The Captain was always chain-smoking a Pall Mall cigarette as he reviewed reports. About halfway into reading, the Captain always wadded the report and threw it, hitting the rookie officer in the chest. A verbal assault about the report then erupted, heavily laced with enough profanity to make a sailor's ears burn. "What are you doing, wasting my time with this garbage? How dare you come into my office and expect me to pass this kind of garbage coming from my shift." About ten minutes later, the rookie was finally dismissed and able to leave with his tail tucked between his legs and almost ready to turn in his badge. He had survived a part of rookie initiation. In defense of Capt. Kelly, rarely did any of his officers ever get embarrassed by a defense attorney on a witness stand because of a poorly drafted report or misspelled words.

Second in command, Lieutenant Harold Engstrom, decided to begin a 'speaker's bureau.' He felt the exposure of officers to young children in a positive light was good public relations for the police department, and talking to children about safety and the dangers of drugs may help them stay safe. Bill was one of the first officers to volunteer to present these programs. In no time, he was visiting elementary schools throughout Beaumont. Bill had a natural rapport with the children he presented programs to. His communication with children pleased the teachers, Lt. Engstrom, and Chief Bauer.

The months and years seemed to fly by. Bill stayed on day shift, working every good and bad part of town. His honesty and integrity earned the respect of his fellow officers as well as many 'bad guys' on the streets. Drug dealers and users that hung out on Irving Street would call the police station asking for Bill. He would call them back a few minutes later on the payphone number they had called him from. The informant would then give Bill information about another drug dealer that was holding dope at that moment, on the same corner or a neighboring corner.

A few minutes later, Bill and his partner would slowly drive by, stop, shake down the suspect, find the dope, and the dealer would be on his way to jail. There was no respect or loyalty amongst drug dealers, especially if a new dealer hoarded on an old dealer's territory.

The largest state fair in Texas sponsored by a non-profit organization is the YMBL (Young Men's Business League) South Texas State Fair, held in Beaumont. Sergeant Bill Reynolds had been a member of the police department for many years. He was assigned to the detective division and was always very distinguished in his daily business attire consisting of a suit or sport coat, tie, and slacks. He had a baritone voice and usually spoke in a slow and definite manner. At the fair, all officers, including Sgt. Reynolds, traded their detective business clothes for their uniform. The police command post at the fair called Bill Davis and Bill Reynolds one evening about a possible drunken male in the patio area. They found the suspect within a matter of minutes. Many of the families on the patio area had moved away from the man who was belligerent and cursing. Reynolds and Davis approached the man and Reynolds began talking to him about his condition. At first, the man appeared to be looking for a fight and Davis was ready to accommodate him. But Reynolds, in his smooth baritone voice, and being the senior officer, took control and began talking to the man and telling him how he (the suspect) really didn't want to fight. Reynolds continued his calming manner with the man. Within a few minutes, the man turned around and let Davis handcuff him. The officers led the man to the command post where an on-duty patrol car was summoned to take him to jail. Before Reynolds and Davis left the command post, the man called to Reynolds and said, "Sgt. Reynolds, I really want to thank you for arresting me. You probably kept me from doing something stupid and I just want to thank you for taking me to jail." Reynolds grinned and told the man it was his pleasure to accommodate him. As the two officers walked back to the patio area, Davis said, "I have now seen it all. I just saw a man thank you for taking him to jail." Reynolds laughed and then said, "I learned a long time ago it is a lot easier to 'talk' someone into jail than to 'fight' them into jail." Davis never forgot Reynolds' statement and tried to use the advice every time he made an arrest throughout his career. Sometimes it worked – sometimes it didn't.

Slowly Bill began to tire of working wrecks and family disturbances. He enjoyed watching many of the department's detectives as they pieced cases together, developed their probable cause, got their warrants, made their arrests, and got confessions from the 'bad guys' for whatever their crimes might be. He began to study. The department was going to give a sergeant's exam in the summer of 1977. He studied night and day for six months. He would have never imagined while going to school that he would study six months for one test, but he was. The test was given and he passed.

Bill's promotion was to take place at 12:01 a.m., October 9, 1977. Like so many other police officers, Bill was working an off-duty extra job that Saturday night at Gerland's Supermarket on N. 11th Street. His job was to walk around the store in plain clothes, looking for shoplifters. At exactly 12:01 a.m. all of the cashiers gathered around

BILL DAVIS

Bill and cheered as he removed his patrol officer's badge from his wallet and replaced it with his shiny new sergeant's badge.

Bill had hired on with Beaumont P.D. with another officer, Frank Coffin, on the same day in June 1972. Both men took the sergeant's test together and were promoted at the same time. Chief Bauer had a standing rule that a detective had to be a sergeant. He also wanted his new sergeants to go straight to the detective division and learn follow-up investigations before they ever thought of being a supervising sergeant in the patrol division. So, the two rookie sergeants reported for duty the following Monday morning to the detective division. Frank was assigned to a veteran detective, Sgt. Ray Cooley. Bill was assigned to another veteran detective, Sgt. Bill Gates. Gates was a great investigator. He had a knack for finding meticulous pieces of evidence and facts in order to put a case together for prosecution. He was a great teacher for his young partner. The two Bills investigated almost every type of crime committed. Davis studied hard and learned fast.

One week after Bill's promotion, the annual South Texas State Fair began. Because of his promotion, Bill literally promoted himself out of a job. The junior officer position with Sgt. Reynolds was for a patrol officer, not another sergeant. About two days before the fair was to begin, Major Cecil Rush called Bill into his office. Major Rush was the Commanding Officer for all the officers working the fair. A new building at the fairgrounds, the coliseum, was going to sell alcohol. By city ordinance, it was going to be the only place on the fairgrounds that a fair patron could go and have a cold beer or a wine cooler. Bill would not be working for the YMBL as other officers were; he would be working for the concessionaire that contracted with the city to run the alcohol concession stand. Maj. Rush advised Bill that he (Bill) would be in charge of all of the officers he recruited to work the coliseum. However, Maj. Rush explained everyone would still answer to him. (After all, he was a Major in rank.) The coliseum quickly became the hangout for anyone wanting a cold beer.

LOOK OUT SATAN ~ GOD'S AT WORK!

Without fail, people drank, tempers flared, and fights broke out. Lots of people went to jail during the fair from the coliseum. Bill had several officers working for him to secure the large-covered facility. One of the officers was his friend, Johnny Vickery. As fights began, Bill never had to worry about where Johnny was, and Johnny never had to worry about where Bill was. They were in some tough fights but always had each other's back.

Sometimes the long fourteen to sixteen-hour days became exhausting, and the officers got a little goofy and played innocent pranks on each other. Bill, Johnny, and the other officers working the coliseum schedule usually stood directly in front of the coliseum's front gate to make sure no one sneaked out of the fenced-in coliseum arena with an alcoholic beverage. There were three flagpoles in front of the main coliseum gate. The flagpoles afforded the officers a great view of patrons going to and from the coliseum, and the poles were a great place to lean against to rest their backs. As an evening wore down and the crowds thinned out, Bill and Johnny would try to be the first ones to calmly ask the other, "Hey, what time is it?" They'd probably been asked that question at least a hundred times that day. Each time, they would pleasantly tell the fair patron the time. But for them, each wore a watch. If either of them wanted to know the time, all they had to do was look at their own wristwatch. The proper reply to the other would have been, "you've got a watch, look for yourself." But the fun was to pull a simple prank on a tired friend, catch him off-guard, and get him to look at his watch and tell the other the time. It was a little inside joke to a couple of trusted friends.

("Hey, Johnny, what time is it?")

Chief Bauer had another standing rule: Become a good investigator in one year. Then, you got transferred. The police department's detective division had evening shift and midnight shift detectives. These detectives worked four ten-hour shifts. Almost to the day of Bill's one-year anniversary to the detective division, he was transferred to the division's midnight shift. He worked Wednesday nights through Saturday nights from 10:00 p.m. to 8:30 a.m. The evening shift detectives worked from 4:00 p.m. to 2:30 a.m. This schedule allowed twice as many detectives on duty during the late-night club hours, when most of the shootings, stabbings, assaults, and murders took place. Bill's partner, who worked the same nights and hours as he did, was Sgt. Walter Billingsley. The supervisor for the evening and midnight shift detectives was Lt. Ed Woodsmall.

After a couple of weeks, Bill settled into his new job. He loved it. This shift gave him the best of patrol work and detective work. If nothing was going on, he would patrol in his plain navy-blue Ford detective car. On many occasions, Bill and Walter would hear a burglary call dispatched and ease into the area with their car lights off. Because detective cars were plain looking and marked patrol cars could be spotted a mile away, they could sneak up on burglars before the 'bad guys' knew they were there. From Thanksgiving to New Year's Eve 1978, Bill and Walter caught more burglars in the act of committing their crimes, than everyone else in the entire police department.

In the 1970s, the 600 Block of Forsythe St. and Shorty's Lounge was noted for shootings, stabbings, prostitution, and drugs. On several occasions Bill got one of his colleagues working midnight patrol to 'stage up' at the police station that was located at 255 College St., about five blocks from 600 Forsythe. Bill notified the dispatcher he would be off the air for a few minutes on Forsythe St. The dispatchers knew what Bill was doing. He covered his police radio so that it could not be seen by anyone looking into his car. He also placed his pistol under his right thigh for quick access. On the second pass driving slowly around the block, one of the ladies of the evening would invariably flag him down. Within seconds to a couple of minutes, she had solicited him for a sexual encounter and named her price. He always told the prostitute he didn't have quite enough money to pay for her services, but he would go to the bank around the corner and cash a check. Everyone knew that

LOOK OUT SATAN ~ GOD'S AT WORK!

American National Bank on Fannin St. in downtown Beaumont was the only bank that had an all-night teller. (Uh, this was before ATMs.) In fact, the regular teller on most of the midnight shifts for the bank was Renee Lane, wife of Sgt. Mike Lane. (Mike was later killed in the line of duty when the helicopter he was riding in crashed in Sabine Lake, September 15, 2004. Mike was a great Christian, husband, father, police officer, pilot, and friend. Mike and Bill joined the department together in June, 1972. He is sorely missed.) Bill always drove to the bank and said "Hello," to Renee. He didn't know if the prostitute's pimp might be following. A few minutes later he slowly drove back to Forsythe St., turning his radio back on, and notifying the patrol officers waiting at the station parking lot to slowly ease to Forsythe St. He advised them to arrest the lady in the red sequin dress (or whatever she might be wearing). He turned the radio off again and slowly drove through the block. The prostitute that had solicited him always flagged him down, thinking she was about to make some fast money. Bill always let her approach the car and began trying to get her to lower her price. While the two were haggling about her price, the patrol car pulled behind his detective car. The two officers walked up, informed the woman she was under arrest for prostitution, put her in their patrol car, and drove away. It was always funny to watch the patrol car turn the corner and drive out of sight. One of the other prostitutes in the area would invariably try and flag Bill down before he drove away, knowing he'd been to the bank and had money. Bill left Forsythe and drove to the police station. The city of Beaumont still operated a jail in the basement of the police station at that time. As he entered the jail, the prostitute always started screaming "I knew you were a cop!" when she saw him. Laughing, he always replied, "If you knew I was a cop, why did you solicit me?" He then finished by booking her in jail. Bill pulled off this type of arrest about once a month. They never learned.

One night, after about a year of Bill being a midnight shift detective, Lt. Woodsmall approached him. "How would you feel about transferring to the Juvenile Bureau?" he asked. "Not no, but uh-uh," he replied. "I want no part of dealing with snotty-nosed brats getting into trouble," Bill said emphatically. A week later, Lt. Woodsmall met with his detective once again. "You've been transferred to the Juvenile Bureau, effective next Monday," Lt. Woodsmall advised. Bill had not applied for the vacancy in the Juvenile Bureau. He did not want the vacancy in the Juvenile Bureau. But, he had no choice. The decision had been made. He was told it was 'for the betterment of the department.' "Yeah right!" Bill said.

The commander of the Juvenile Bureau was Bill's old friend, Lt. Harold Engstrom. As Bill reported for duty, Harold told Bill that he had specifically hand-picked him. Bill told his friend he did not want to be there. He emphatically told his new commander that he did not want to deal with 'snotty-nosed brats.' "Up here," Harold said, "we deal with two kinds of investigations. One type of investigation is where the juvenile gets into trouble. The other type of investigation is where someone commits a crime against a child – child physical and child sexual abuse crimes." "You mean I can put adults in jail for hurting or molesting little children?" Bill inquired. "Yep," was Harold's emphatic reply. This transfer may not be too bad, Bill thought. One of the things Bill really despised was someone hurting or sexually molesting an innocent, helpless little child. "If this means I can put 'bad guys' in jail, then I'm your man," Bill told his boss. Within a week, Bill was assigned almost every investigation for physical and sexual abuse to a child that happened within the city limits of Beaumont. At the time Bill made his commitment to Harold, he did not know that commitment would take him through thousands of child abuse and sex crime investigations, and a lifetime commitment to protecting children. It took Bill a while to realize that God was at work and all of this was a part of His plan for Bill.

The years continued on as Bill devoted his life to saving innocent, abused children. He poured himself into case after case, solving each one if the facts and evidence were there. It didn't take him long to realize how complex these investigations were. It was one thing to investigate a crime with adults involved, but it was quite another thing to investigate a crime where the victim(s) or witnesses were children. Many of these children were infants and could not tell their stories of victimization. Some cases Bill investigated involved unborn children. He developed a philosophy over the years – that he was the only person on this earth that could possibly help this child out of a 'hell on earth' situation. Some people would think this philosophy was arrogant. But after analyzing this thought, they would realize that Bill (or whoever the detective might be for any investigation) was the only one in charge of the investigation. If he failed to solve a case for a child (or whoever the victim might be), he may have caused more problems for that child (or victim) than if the investigation had never taken place. Therefore, if at all possible, he had to solve each case because a child's life was in the balance. Bill tried to instill this philosophy in every officer that attended the child abuse core course he taught at the Lamar Regional Law Enforcement Academy for over thirty years.

One day Bill was called to St. Elizabeth Hospital to investigate a case of possible physical abuse to a child involving a little seven-month-old boy. Ms. Smith, the child's paternal grandmother, was a nurse's aide at the hospital. Her son was in the U.S. Air Force and was stationed at Dyess Air Force Base near Abilene, Texas. He had married a lady from the Southeast Texas area and their only child was this little boy. The young family came to town for a weekend visit. When little Johnny needed his diaper changed, Ms. Smith was the typical grandmother. She volunteered to change Johnny's diaper, giving her more contact and quality time with her grandson. As she began changing her grandson's diaper, she noticed that he would cry every time she moved his right thigh. There was no bruising on Johnny's right thigh, but it was swollen almost twice the size of the left thigh. Being around doctors and nurses every day at work told her that something was not right with her grandson. She immediately carried him to the Emergency Department at St. Elizabeth's.

The hospital radiologist immediately observed that Johnny's right femur was fractured. He also noticed that the right femur had been fractured on a prior occasion. Further x-rays also showed that the left femur and the right humerus near the shoulder joint had been broken on prior occasions. The emergency department doctors now decided to do a complete battery of tests on this baby that was possibly an abused child. Tests revealed that the little boy was blind in his right eye. The doctors surmised the blindness was caused by blows in and around the right eye. He also had a cataract in his left eye that would possibly cause him to go blind in the near future. Bill arrived at the hospital and the doctor in charge of Johnny filled the detective in as to the old and new injuries they had found so far. The doctor advised that he ordered a series of blood tests on the baby to check for further indications of abuse.

Bill finished taking notes from his interview with the doctor and walked down the emergency department hallway to the baby's room. A nurse was holding Johnny's little hand and softly talking to him as he lay on his back on the hospital bed. A lab technician entered the room just prior to Bill's entry. She was there to draw blood from Johnny so the tests the doctor ordered could be completed. As her needle penetrated his little body, Bill observed something he had never seen in his entire life. This seven-month-old baby did not cry. He did not automatically begin crying as babies and little ones do when they get a shot at the doctor's office, or when they suddenly feel pain. He did not look where the needle was piercing his body. Instead, this little boy looked straight at the ceiling. His little eyes never veered from a spot on the ceiling the entire time the nurse was filling her vials with his blood. She slowly removed the needle and put a comic character band-aid on his 'bo-bo.' He slowly moved his gaze from the ceiling to looking at the people in his room. Bill later surmised that little Johnny had learned in his short seven months of life, that if you felt pain, you had better not cry out, or more pain would come.

Bill worked frantically with two deputies from the Taylor County Sheriff's Department in Abilene, Texas to solve this case. The Beaumont Police Department had to be involved in this case because Bill had the child in the hospital in Beaumont, but all of little Johnny's injuries allegedly occurred in Taylor County. The deputies and Bill learned that on several occasions, Johnny's parents would get into an argument which would turn physical. His father would beat his mother and then storm out of their small mobile home. Their fighting would cause them to slam into Johnny's baby bed, startling him and causing him to cry. After being physically beaten and emotionally distraught, his mother dealt with his crying by grabbing him out of his baby bed by one of his thighs or upper arms and fling him across the mobile home where he would hit one of the walls and fall to the floor. Both parents were arrested and Johnny's mother was tried in Beaumont, found guilty, and sentenced to eighteen years in prison. His father was tried in Abilene. He was found guilty but was only given probation because he did not actually cause any of Johnny's injuries. He knew about the injuries his wife was causing to the child but he did nothing to either stop her or get Johnny medical help. In addition to probation, he was dishonorably discharged from the Air Force. Child Protective Services investigated the paternal grandmother and awarded custody of Johnny to her.

One of the top institutes of higher learning for law enforcement officers has always been Sam Houston State University located in Huntsville, Texas. Their criminal justice department has been touted as one of the best in the nation. Lt. Weldon Dunlap, the new supervisor for the Juvenile Bureau, heard of a two-day child abuse seminar at the university. The speaker was a retired Los Angeles police officer who traveled throughout the country educating officers about child abuse. Lt. Dunlap decided his two top child abuse detectives, Bill Davis and Bill Jordan, needed to attend the seminar. The two detectives arrived at the university dormitory room assigned to them on Sunday afternoon, February 13, 1983. The seminar began the next morning, Valentine's Day, as Jim Mead, a child abuse detective recently retired from L.A.P.D., introduced himself. He was a stocky, balding man with a natural ability to command one's attention. The classroom was full of officers from agencies throughout Texas. They had all come together to learn how to better investigate crimes committed against 'the most innocent of the innocent.'

Most in-service seminars, no matter what the occupation, were usually boring. The two days of this seminar flew by. Bill made notes throughout the child abuse binder he and other officers received at the beginning of the seminar. Bill had already seen many of the physical abuse indicators, neglect and emotional maltreatment issues, and sexual molestation facts that were discussed in the seminar from the cases he investigated in almost four years of being a child abuse detective. Jim Mead's seminar reinforced and clarified many of the issues Bill had seen in prior cases.

The seminar was finally over and the two detectives headed for Beaumont in Jordan's detective car. As Bill Jordan drove, Bill Davis sat on the passenger's side staring out the window. The old information Bill Davis knew and the new information he'd learned in the seminar kept playing over and over in his head. Bill realized that every time a case folder was laid on his desk for him to solve, he was too late for that victim listed on the 'offense report' form. He had not prevented the incident being reported for him to investigate from happening to that victim. There had to be a better way to protect innocent children and rape victims. That quiet, small voice started speaking to Bill again. It kept saying "You can do what Jim Mead does. You can tell people about child abuse. You can tell people what to look for in physical and sexual abuse to children incidents. You can reach more people with your voice than on a case-by-case basis. Tell the people what to look for. Tell the people to listen to the children."

LOOK OUT SATAN ~ GOD'S AT WORK!

Bill arrived for work on Wednesday morning. He poured his usual cup of black coffee and sauntered down the hallway to Lt. Dunlap's office. "How was the seminar?" Weldon asked. Bill told him how great it was. As the two talked, Bill poured out his thoughts to his boss. "I want to put a seminar together and present it to officers, CPS investigators, and people in the community," Bill said. "If we can teach more people what to look for, we can have more eyes watching and helping to protect children," Bill stated. "I think it's a great idea," Weldon replied. "You put it together and I'll help you present it. Just be sure to keep up with your cases," his boss warned. "I will," Bill stated and left for his office. His head was spinning with ideas. Bill didn't know where this idea was going to take him, but he was excited. He didn't know he was about to invest hundreds, even thousands of hours of his own time making this program (and many others) a reality. Throughout the years, Beaumont P.D. never asked Bill to develop and present any of his programs. But, the department didn't need to. That quiet, small voice inside Bill's head, the Holy Spirit, kept telling Bill, "Keep going! Keep presenting! You have lives to save!"

"Whatever you do, do it enthusiastically, as something done for the Lord and not for men, knowing that you will receive the reward of an inheritance from the Lord – you serve the Lord Christ." Colossians 3:23-24 Standard Bible

Johnny & Pat Long

Bill's first photo as a Beaumont Police Officer, taken June 1972 for his police identification card.

Chapter Seven

A Program Is Born

"Now He who supplies seed to the sower and bread for food will also supply and increase your store of seed and will enlarge the havest of your righteousness." II Corinthians 9:10 (NIV)

[Just as God provides seed for the farmer, he also supplies us with seed {precious gifts} to invest into the lives of others. It is His good will for us to experience increase in our lives. The potential for an awesome harvest rests within the seed {the gift}, but it cannot bring forth the desired result until it is deposited. May God grant us the wisdom to take what has been placed in our grasp and invest it wisely. Then, we might see a harvest of 30, 60, or 100 fold. So, INCREASE! [Neal Payne]

PowerPoint had not yet been invented. Slides of pictures placed in a round carousel on top of a slide projector was the video tool of the day. This technology was placed on the market in 1962 by Kodak and was the way video presentations were presented in the 1960s and 1970s. Bill left Weldon's office and walked to the main level of the police station to the Training Division. If anyone could get Bill started on putting a slide presentation together, it was Sgt. Robert Shiflet. 'Bob' was in his office and Bill began telling him about his ideas. When he finished, Bob began to formulate Bill's seminar. He would need lots of poster paper. Bob then introduced Bill to a croytape machine. This machine would print letters on a clear piece of tape. The tape backing was pulled off and the tape was then pasted onto poster paper. Bob loaned Bill an extra 35mm camera and showed Bill how to photograph the poster paper with the pasted letters. The film would be processed, and, instead of photos, tiny slides would be made. It was that easy. Bob also loaned him a Kodak slide carousel projector and one 140-slot round carousel to put his slides in as he had them developed. Bill was now in business. If this seminar idea was to become reality, it was now up to him and no one else.

Bill's office soon began to look like an arts and crafts room. He came in early almost every day and worked on putting slides together. He could see that he would need lots of slides because child abuse is a very complex issue. Bill realized he would need to break his seminar into two major parts - physical abuse and sexual abuse. He saw the necessity to include a minor but important third part - dealing with physical neglect and emotional maltreatment. He also knew from experience that viewing a bunch of slides with lots of words would get boring very quickly. He began to reflect on many of the cases he investigated during the last four years. He reviewed some of the more memorable cases and selected photographs of specific injuries. Bill's process was to emphasize an issue or thought with words emboldened on a piece of poster paper, photograph the poster, and develop the photograph into a slide. There is great truth in the saying, 'a picture is worth a thousand words.' Bill knew the slides would get his point across to the audience much better if he stated the law or an abuse indicator on a slide, and then follow that slide with a photo slide of the actual injury he was trying to explain to his audience. He also had to be careful not to show the identity of victims in these photo slides. Some of the cases these photos represented were still pending and awaiting court disposition.

There was simply no photograph available to show some of the issues and facts that Bill wanted to convey to future audiences. He went to Lt. Pat O'Quinn's office in the Detective Division. Everyone knew Pat was an exceptional artist. For Pat, painting was strictly a hobby, a past-time. He was very good at it. At one point in Pat's painting career, he was commissioned by an East Texas attorney to

LOOK OUT SATAN ~ GOD'S AT WORK!

paint the last battle at the Alamo. This attorney had done extensive research on the battles at the Alamo. To this point, no one had ever painted a true rendition of the last battle. With research and ideas in hand, the attorney and Pat began to formulate the painting. When the oil painting was finished, it was truly a work of art. The painting depicted the last battle at the Alamo so realistically and historically true, that Pat's painting had the honor of being displayed inside the Alamo for a period of time. Bill explained his endeavor to Pat. Bill told him of his dilemma where some ideas needed a drawing or sketch when no photo was available. Pat was glad to help.

Bill now seemed to have all of the ingredients needed to put his seminar together. Having majored in business administration at ETBC, he took accounting and economics courses at college. However, Bill never got around to taking the marketing classes before leaving ETBC and returning to Southeast Texas. Bill realized two things. The program needed to be marketed. He needed to be marketed, too. People needed to know who he was and his area of expertise. But God was in control. God was slowly putting everything in place for Bill to market child abuse awareness and himself to others. Bill was learning how to be factual and honest but without bragging in his description of himself. He was learning how to go forth boldly with his facts and information about child abuse and the program God was charging him to present. The days turned into weeks and weeks into months. The slide carousel began to fill with slides reflecting the grim story of child abuse. A target date of Thursday, July 28, 1983, was set. God was in control.

Bill considered various titles for his seminar but nothing seemed to work. Child abuse was a topic that his parents and grandparents would have never discussed. It was an issue in time that was never talked about. In fact, children were basically considered property of parents and could be dealt with as parents saw fit. In many situations where a child was removed from a parent's home due to abuse, the placement home was far worse than the abusive home. As society became more informed through television, people began to see that child abuse was rampant throughout the United States. People began talking about the atrocities of hurting and molesting children. Bill was riding in his detective car one day thinking about new slides he needed for his program. That quiet, small voice inside of Bill said five words: "Child Abuse: A National Epidemic." God had given Bill the title for the seminar. The 'glass houses' where abuse was occurring were about to be smashed.

Flyers about the seminar were made and posted around the police station, entitled 'Child Abuse: A National Epidemic.' Flyers were also sent to neighboring law enforcement agencies and local Child Protective Services offices in Jefferson County and neighboring counties, advertising for their investigators to attend the program. Weldon was going to present the physical abuse portion of the program and Bill was going to present the neglect, emotional, and sexual portion of the presentation. The patrol squad room in the police station's basement was the location for the program.

Bill had no idea how many people would show up. He and Weldon decided the seminar should be an 8:00 a.m. to 5:00 p.m. presentation. They arrived early that morning. People began arriving as early as 7:30 a.m. and soon were filling up the squad room. More chairs were brought to the room to accommodate everyone. In all, eighty-five people attended the seminar. Bill was elated with the response. At 8:00 a.m., Weldon promptly welcomed everyone to the seminar. He began his presentation by showing the slides Bill put together on physical abuse. Weldon was basically a quiet person and his presentation was quite informative, but it was presented in Weldon's mild manner of speaking. Everyone was taking notes and seemed to absorb the information. The seminar was a great way of getting the many people who become involved in these types of investigations to all be on the same page. Weldon finished and everyone left for lunch. The afternoon belonged to Bill.

Everyone came back for the afternoon session and Bill began

his segment of the seminar. Within a couple of minutes, Bill was on a roll. He was in front of an audience. He was suddenly pouring out his heart and soul to a room full of people. He didn't need a microphone. The slides were his notes. He didn't need a podium. He was moving in front of the audience, changing slides, pointing out specific issues or facts with a pointer, and emotionally motivating everyone. His presentation was not of the Sunday school nature. It was a hell-fire and brimstone sermon. Sweat was pouring down his face as he compelled his audience to engage in his philosophy that they were the only ones that could help deliver an abused child from a living hell. Finally, it was 5:00 p.m. and his part was over. One of the homicide/robbery detectives, Sgt. Eddie McDonald walked up to Bill and said, "If I didn't know better, I'd swear I was just in church." Bill thanked his friend and started putting away the equipment used for the seminar. Eddie was a revered homicide/robbery detective. For him to take the time to compliment Bill's presentation was very special. It would take several more years for Eddie's statement to really sink into Bill's head and heart. As the saying goes, a snowball starts downhill slowly and then picks up speed. As he toted the equipment back to a corner of his office, Bill was elated with the way the seminar went. He hoped he would get the chance to present the program again. It was fun and it felt natural like Bill belonged in front of an audience. July 28, 1983, was the first and last time Weldon presented any part of this seminar.

People who attended the seminar evidently talked to others about how good the child abuse presentation was. In October, Bill was asked to present a two-hour version of the eight-hour seminar to a group of adults who were involved with pre-school children. It was his second opportunity to speak to a group of people about child abuse. The group was a small one. Bill poured his heart out as he shared highlights from the full program into a two-hour time slot.

He could have easily said that only five or ten people in an audience was not worth his time. But, that quiet, small voice always spoke to Bill at the right moment. He remembered one time as the quiet, gentle voice of God spoke, telling him that someone in that small group of one, two, or five people attending his seminar may be the one person who would save a child's life in the future. So, no matter how big or small the crowd, Bill always gave one-hundred percent of himself to the audience.

The holidays came and went in 1983. Word was spreading about this child abuse seminar and the highly motivated detective who presented it. He thought of several more slides that needed to be added to the program and he continued to come in early several mornings a week to work on them.

Deer season was over. Bill and his friend, Ron, decided to get away for the weekend and go squirrel hunting. Bill and Ron packed Bill's truck, along with Bill's four-legged best friend, BeBe, and headed to their hunting lease north of Spurger. The next morning, January 7, 1984, at 7:05 a.m., Bill's world was totally and completely turned upside down.

Sgt. Davis addressing an audience as the keynote speaker after receiving the Kinder Award in Houston, Texas, February 22, 2001.

Chapter Eight

Just Getting Started

"For God's gifts and His call are irrevocable. He never withdraws them when once they are given and he does not change His mind about those to whom He gives His grace or to whom He sends His call." Romans 11:29 – The Amplified Bible

Bill was still recuperating in February 1984. He received a call from his friend, Don Raiford, Director of the Lamar Institute of Technology Regional Police Academy. Don was a member of the Beaumont Police Department before taking the director's job at the police academy. Don and Bill patrolled the streets of Beaumont on many shifts together in the 1970s when they were both riding patrol. Don was a tall, quiet guy, but one heck of a scrapper when things got tough. Don called his friend, first to see how he was doing from his gunshot wound. Then, he inquired about the upcoming week-long child abuse seminar that was scheduled to start on February 20th. The seminar was placed on the calendar before the Christmas holidays. He informed Bill the seminar could be rescheduled. "Nope," Bill replied, "My hand and arm are hurt, not my mouth. I'll put the program on wearing my bandages and sling." Bill checked with Weldon to make sure he was not violating any department policy by presenting the seminar at the police academy while still off work due to his injury. "As long as you don't put in for pay or compensatory time," Weldon explained, "you can do the program." It was a done deal. The show went on. That day, fifteen police officers from around the area listened intently as Bill taught them the signs to look for in abused children and how to save their lives.

Eight weeks after the gunshot injury, Bill was back at work.

LOOK OUT SATAN ~ GOD'S AT WORK!

He had a mountain of child abuse cases to solve. Some of the cases waited eight weeks for him to finish investigating. The children in these cases were being protected by Child Protective Services through relative placement or foster care placement until he could return to work, finish the investigation, and file the case with the district attorney's office for prosecution. More pressing cases were re-assigned to other detectives when a child appeared to be in grave danger in their abusive situation. Word was spreading that Bill was back and the phone was ringing with requests for his program.

Bill fulfilled his two-hour speaking obligation to the Southeast Texas Association for the Education of Children on March 22nd. In April, Bill spoke to a social studies class at South Park High School. In May, he presented child abuse programs at the District 4 PTA Annual Spring Conference at the 'Holidome' Holiday Inn in Beaumont. In June, Bill presented his first program for volunteers with Southeast Texas Rape Crisis Center. (To date, Bill still volunteers for the Southeast Texas Rape & Suicide Crisis Center, presenting two to four programs per year for this important organization.) In July, another eight-hour seminar was presented at the regional police academy. This time, fifty-five officers from throughout the region listened as Bill taught them how to save a child's life.

Bill was really enjoying his new role as an educator. Bill began investigating child abuse cases in 1979. Since that time, he investigated hundreds of child abuse cases, more than anyone else in the region. Now he was taking this knowledge and experience and sharing it with fellow officers. Some of these officers were from other departments and worked very few child abuse cases. Bill's seminar, with his knowledge, experience, and passion, helped them work through their investigations with greater skill when the occasion arose in their jurisdiction. Bill's seminar also helped officers satisfy bi-annual in-service training requirements.

A representative from Anahuac Elementary School called Bill.

BILL DAVIS

The school's PTA and faculty wanted him to present his two-hour child abuse program on Tuesday, September 18, 1984. The police department's crime prevention unit was located down the hallway from Bill's office. Lt. Ed Woodsmall was no longer the evening/midnight shift detective supervisor. He was leading a new crime prevention awareness unit within the police department. Two of the officers in the unit were Officer Billy Blankenship and Officer Jim Carpenter. These two officers developed a series of puppet shows, and they had just recently obtained a 'McGruff the Crime Dog' costume. McGruff was quickly gaining popularity in safety programs and Billy and Jim enjoyed their new costume as they traveled to various elementary schools presenting an array of safety topics to the students. Bill asked Billy to accompany him to the program in Anahuac. The plan was for Billy to put on a puppet show to start the program and then Bill would present his two-hour child abuse awareness program.

The two officers arrived in Anahuac and Billy set up the puppet stage while Bill set up his slide projector. The school bell rang and they could hear children scurrying through the hallways, making their way to the carpool or buses to go home. Several PTA members arrived and introduced themselves to Bill and Billy. Teachers began arriving as soon as the hallways cleared. Billy presented a cute puppet show for the grown-ups. He was showing them one of the programs he would show their children if they invited him back to their school. Then, it was Bill's turn. He poured his heart out to these parents and teachers, showing them through his slides and words how people hurt children and how they could help save them. His program was over at 5:30 p.m. The teachers and parents thanked the two officers for coming and left the school. Most of the participants in the audience were women and they had families waiting at home for them to cook supper.

Bill and Billy loaded their equipment in Bill's detective car and headed east on IH-10 back to Beaumont. They were pretty quiet as they rode down the freeway. It had been a long day. Billy broke the silence as he continued staring down the freeway and said, "You know, you're doing a great job educating grown-ups about child abuse, but you're not doing one thing about educating potential victims – the children." Bill was so proud of his work. But in one statement, Billy brought him to reality. Billy revealed a gaping hole in Bill's efforts to save children's lives and educate them, too. Billy continued, "You could talk to them about bicycle safety, sitting in their car seats, and good touches and bad touches. Heck, you can even talk to them about gun safety." Bill didn't say a word. He was too busy driving and thinking. God had just spoken to him through Billy, and he knew it. Bill was learning not to ignore God when He talked to him like this. The slides for the children were already formulating in Bill's mind. This trip was the only time Bill and Billy ever did a program together. God used the moment to plant a seed. Once again, God was busy at work.

Bill arrived for work Wednesday with a new project on his agenda. He began planning how he would present his own safety program to children. He presented a lot of programs ten years earlier with Lt. Engstrom and the police department speaker's bureau. However, this would be his personal program for children. He knew that the attention span for most children, especially in the younger ages, was about thirty minutes. He began outlining his program. He decided he would only talk to the children for the first part of the program and use posters for the 'good touch-bad touch' finale.

His first opportunity to present his new program for children was at the invitation of Mount Calvary Baptist Church in Beaumont. He began his program talking about gun safety. He showed the children his hand and arm as he talked to them about gun safety. He talked about bicycle safety and the importance of sitting in their car seats. He asked the children to be his helpers, making sure that moms, dads, grandparents, and big brothers and sisters also wore their seat belts. He talked to them about not stealing and not taking drugs. For many years, Bill carried a police department drug display to show to children. All of the children were intrigued with the chicken foot marijuana pipe that was on display. He ended the program talking about sexual abuse on a level children could understand. Bill encouraged the children to tell someone they trusted if someone ever touched them in a way or on a place on their body that made them feel uncomfortable. He also reassured the children that if this ever happened to them, that they had done nothing wrong. The adults in the church were not used to seeing this side of a police officer. They were impressed at how his words dropped to a level that the children could understand. Bill received high marks for his new program's first presentation. Requests began pouring in from throughout the Southeast Texas area for not only the child abuse program but also the child safety program.

After about the third or fourth request for programs, Bill began keeping a record of where he presented a program and its date, the group or person that requested the program, and the number of people who attended the program. From July 28, 1983 to December 31, 1984, Bill presented his two programs to 1,332 people.

One of the last programs he presented for the year was on December 6, 1984, at the Hilton Hotel in Beaumont. He was a member of a four-member panel discussing child abuse in Southeast Texas. The Beaumont Chamber of Commerce – Leadership Beaumont Crime Group sponsored the event. It was attended by over one-hundred people from various occupations and included concerned parents and grandparents from the community. The panel members were The Honorable Judge James Farris from the family district court at the Jefferson County Courthouse, Dr. Curt Wills a local psychologist, Ms. Karen McClain with Child Protective Services, and Bill. The program included a question-and-answer period from the audience. One man in the audience became quite irate and demanded a specific answer to a pending child abuse case. No one could give specific answers to the man's questions because no one on the panel was involved in his investigation. Several uniformed

LOOK OUT SATAN ~ GOD'S AT WORK!

Beaumont P.D. officers got up from their chairs in the audience and began slowly moving toward the man. While the man's focus was on the panel members and his questions, he had quietly been surrounded by six Beaumont police officers sitting beside and in back of him, just in case. Judge Tom Maness, District Attorney for Jefferson County rose from his seat. He resolved the stalemate the man caused by asking the man to meet with him after the symposium, and he would personally look into the man's allegations. The situation created by the man was defused and other audience members participated in the discussion.

After the panel adjourned, a man from the audience walked up to Bill and introduced himself. He was the news director for KBMT-TV Channel 12 in Beaumont and he was also a member of the Leadership Beaumont Group. He and other members of the Leadership group observed Bill's slide presentation in a workshop with Bill before the panel discussion. He and the others noticed that Bill's information through the slides was well laid out, but the makeup of the slides was crude. (What can one expect from poster paper, a croytape machine, and a camera?) He had a proposal for Bill. The Leadership group wanted to fund the cost of bringing Bill's slides to a professional level. Two of the people in the Leadership group who were going to help Bill upgrade his slides were involved with Channel 12. The full-time employee with Channel 12 was a man named Chris Bishop. The other person worked part-time with Channel 12 and was Chris's wife, Denise. Bill could hardly believe what he was hearing. He was going to have all of his slides brought to the same professional level as programs presented by major corporations – free! And when Bill heard who would be helping him, he was almost speechless. Chris and Denise lived across the street and two doors down from his house on Cherry Drive. They worked feverishly to upgrade all of Bill's slides. All he could think of was wow! God's at work – again!

That quiet, soft voice continued to talk to Bill. Many times he didn't understand why, but he listened. The police department originally paid for the photo development of Bill's slides using poster paper and the croytape machine. The new professional slides were being paid for by an outside agency. These new slides were being done for Bill, not the police department. This meant that these slides and this program belonged to him, not the police department, nor the city. Bill didn't think much of it, but that little voice quietly whispered that from this moment on, all slides would be paid for by Bill, or someone helping him, and not the department.

"Some day, you will leave the department and take this program with you," the little voice said. "Don't let someone claim that it belongs to the department." As new slides were made throughout the years, the department never paid for any of them.

Bill came up with another huge idea. He wanted to put his child abuse program on in grand scale for the entire community. He discussed the idea with Weldon. Bill thought the Julie Rogers Theatre would be a great location for the program. They might be able to get the theatre for free since it was owned by the city. Bill thought he might be able to get some donations for posters to advertise the seminar. He explained that the seminar would be great for public relations for the police department. Weldon liked the idea and would present the proposal to Chief Bauer. A couple of days later, Weldon told Bill the chief had given his blessing.

Bill contacted the person in charge of the Julie Rogers Theatre at city hall. The theatre was available on January 14, 1985. Bill was a city employee with a grand idea for saving children's lives in Southeast Texas. There would be no charge. Chris and Denise now had a deadline. Both wanted the new slides ready for the big show. The problem was that Bill kept coming up with ideas for new slides. Bill contacted Pat O'Quinn and requested more drawings for more slides. He also reviewed more old investigations and found additional photos of injuries that could be used in the seminar. The program was growing.

Local radio and television stations gave Bill free advertisement

LOOK OUT SATAN ~ GOD'S AT WORK!

for his seminar. All of the television stations promised they would be on hand the night of the program. The night finally arrived. Bill wanted to start the program with a bang. One of Bill's fellow officers, SWAT team member, and good friend was Jimmy Singletary. Jimmy loved martial arts and studied under Mr. Fred Simon, a local elementary school teacher and a sixth-degree black belt in Tae-kwon-do. Mr. Fred was a large black man with a barrel-chested build and a quick smile. He was loved by his students and their instructor loved them. Mr. Fred had a beautiful baritone voice and he loved to sing. The program opened with Mr. Fred singing our National Anthem – acappella. He received a standing ovation.

Bill thanked everyone for their attendance and then told everyone he was sad they felt the need to be there. He explained it was saddening that child abuse existed in the greatest country in the world. Bill began his slide show, speaking with a passion and fire that many people in the audience had never experienced. Sweat poured from his face as he showed slide after slide, with no one leaving. Two-and-one-half-hours later, Bill showed his last slide. It was a cartoon drawing of four children – a white boy, a white girl, a boy of color, and a girl of color. He challenged everyone in the audience, "If we as adults don't protect our children, our greatest resource, my question for tonight is – Who will?" Over 450 people filled the Julie Rogers Theatre that night.

Officer Bill presented his 'Child Safty: First & Forever with Officer Bill' program to his granddaughter, Kaelyn's, pre-kindergarten class. She is helping her PawPaw hand out 'Officer Bill's Junior Officer' sticker badges.

Most of Kaelyn's classmates wore their paper police caps to the program in honor of Officer Bill and all law enforcement officers.

Officer Bill visited an elementary school and a group of the students presented blank sheets of paper to Bill for his autograph.

Children are very attentive as Officer Bill discusses safety issues with them that could save their life during his 'Child Safety: First & Forever with Officer Bill' program.

Chapter Nine

Faith vs. Fear

"For God hath not given us the spirit of fear, but of power, and of love, and of a sound mind." II Timothy 1:7 – King James Version

The seminar at the Julie Rogers Theatre was a great catalyst for Bill's programs. Calls came in from throughout Southeast Texas. Bill was speaking about child abuse to audiences at least one or more times per week. By the time 1985 ended, Bill had presented forty-six programs to over 6,000 people. He also received an invitation to become a member of a state organization called the Texas Committee for the Prevention of Child Abuse and Neglect. (The organization shortened their name many years later to Prevent Child Abuse Texas. PCAT was one of the leading non-profit organizations in Texas promoting child abuse awareness and intervention. Its longtime director retired, and sadly, the organization folded a short time later.) Bill gladly accepted the invitation. This organization would help him see the state and national situation dealing with child abuse. One of their first undertakings was to sponsor and coordinate a child abuse conference for law enforcement officers, CPS investigators, and others involved with child abuse situations. The conference was held in January 1986, and the response to the conference was above and beyond all expectations. Bill was one of the conference workshop presenters and was excited to be part of the experience. (The PCAT conference continued for over twenty-five years. Bill was a workshop speaker every year. He was a keynote speaker for the conference on two occasions.)

The state conference gave Bill statewide exposure. He began to receive invitations to speak at various locations throughout Texas.

BILL DAVIS

Even though the police department enjoyed the wonderfully positive publicity Bill's programs brought to the city and the department, Weldon made it very clear that any program Bill presented outside the Southeast Texas area was on his time, not the city's time. Every program Bill presented outside the area cost him money, not the city. Throughout his entire career with the police department, Bill always used his vacation time or compensatory time in order to fulfill his out-of-the-area speaking obligations. But that didn't matter. His passion was to save children's lives and through his investigations, his programs became stronger by the day. Listening to that quiet, small voice, Bill slowly realized that God had given him a special calling. When he was in college, he worried that he attended college on a ministerial scholarship, yet he wasn't preaching. He began presenting programs to children while he was a patrol officer. Now, through his experience and expertise as a child abuse and sex crimes detective, he was presenting child abuse awareness seminars and programs throughout Texas. He was presenting his children's program, *'Child Safety: First & Forever with Officer Bill,'* to elementary children. He was slowly realizing that God made him a minister with a very unique ministry.

    Bill was driving in the north end of Beaumont one day when he drove past his church, North End Baptist Church. He saw his pastor's vehicle beside the church and drove into the parking lot. Brother Harold Halcomb was always busy doing God's work and Bill decided he needed to tell his pastor and next-door neighbor something. He entered Bro. Halcomb's office and the two men exchanged pleasantries. Bill then shared his thoughts with his pastor. He told Bro. Halcomb that many people live their entire life without realizing their purpose in life. For many years Bill wondered if he was doing God's will. He felt God calling him to be a preacher in high school and he preached almost one-hundred youth sermons. And, he'd gone to a Baptist college on a ministerial scholarship, but he never preached a sermon. Bill then shared with Bro. Halcomb that his 'church' was every location where he was asked to present a program and his 'congregation' was every school, conference, or seminar where he was asked to present one of the programs God gave him to present. Bro. Halcomb smiled and acknowledged Bill's statement saying, "It's a satisfying feeling, isn't it?"

Several weeks later, Bill parked in the back parking lot of the police station and climbed the steps going to the building's back door. As he reached the top steps, he recognized Haskell Taylor, the Texas Ranger assigned to the Texas Department of Public Safety Beaumont office, as he was exiting the building. The two lawmen exchanged handshakes and greetings. Haskell mentioned that he was working with some of the homicide detectives on a murder investigation. Bill had worked a couple of child abuse and sex crime investigations with the Texas Ranger and greatly admired him as an individual. Bill also admired Haskell as being a part of the 'best known' law enforcement agency in the world – the Texas Rangers. Suddenly, Haskell asked Bill, "Have you ever thought of being a Texas Ranger?" Without hesitation Bill excitedly said, "Of course! What law enforcement officer hasn't? But, you have to be a DPS (Texas Department of Public Safety) trooper to go into the Rangers." "Well, there have been times where outstanding investigators have been sponsored by a Ranger and have become a Ranger," Haskell explained. Bill didn't say anything. He wasn't sure where this conversation was going. "I've been watching you through the years. You are a meticulous investigator, a great speaker, and a positive image for the police department. You would be an asset to the Texas Rangers. If you are interested, I will sponsor you." Bill was speechless. He didn't know what to say. This man Bill so admired had just invited him to be a part of the greatest law enforcement organization in the world. Haskell had just invited Bill to consider joining an organization with many fine Rangers in their department at that time such as Haskell himself, Ranger Glenn Elliott in East Texas, and Ranger H. Joaquin Jackson in Southwest Texas. Bill finally found his voice and thanked Haskell for an unbelievable honor. He would have to talk to his family and get back to him. With that, they shook hands and went their separate ways. Wow, the possibility of being a Texas Ranger! Bill was totally overwhelmed. He didn't get a thing accomplished the rest of the day!

A few weeks later, Bill called Haskell. He thanked him again for the great honor of being considered for the possibility of becoming a Texas Ranger. He admitted, though, that being a Ranger and being stationed somewhere in Texas, probably away from the Beaumont area would create a hardship on not just him, but also his entire family. With great reluctance, Bill declined the invitation. Haskell thanked Bill for his phone call and his honesty. It was a decision Bill somewhat regretted. He had just given up the possibility of being a Texas Ranger. He realized he would never have this opportunity again in his life. He felt God would have blessed him in that endeavor, had he pursued it. He felt God would not have allowed that door to open had it not been okay with Him. But, even though it may have been okay with God, Bill felt the path he was on was the one most approved by God. Bill felt there was so much more he needed to accomplish concerning child abuse awareness and saving children's lives.

Chief Bauer retired in 1984, after serving as police chief longer than any other chief prior to him. The city decided to look outside the ranks of the police department and found a man named John Swan from Kansas City, Missouri. Chief Swan took over the helm of the department and just as any new chief would do, he began making changes within the department that he felt would improve the department's ability to protect the city and enforce the law. He had everyone in the department write their job duties and these documents were forwarded to him. Bill not only described his job as a child abuse detective, but he also described how he put a program together that was now receiving local and statewide exposure. Chief Swan stopped Bill in the hallway one day and inquired about his seminar. Bill was honored that the new chief would ask about this endeavor.

LOOK OUT SATAN ~ GOD'S AT WORK!

"Let me know when you are going to present your next seminar locally," Chief Swan said. "I want to see it." A couple of weeks later, Bill informed the chief of an upcoming seminar that would be in town. The chief thanked him and Bill figured that was the end of it. On the day of the presentation, Bill was setting up equipment to conduct his program and was surprised to see Chief Swan walk into the building. He stayed throughout Bill's presentation. At the conclusion of the program, Chief Swan came up to Bill and complimented him on an outstanding presentation.

Approximately one week later, Bill arrived for work on a Monday morning. He went to his office and as was his habit, got his coffee cup, went to the restroom, and washed it out. He went to the coffee pot and poured himself a cup of black coffee. One of his fellow detectives walked to the coffee pot and also poured himself a cup of coffee. He congratulated Bill on his transfer and asked him how he felt about it. "What transfer?" Bill asked in surprise. He immediately went to Lt. Dunlap's office, wanting to know what was going on. Bill was informed by the lieutenant that Chief Swan had liked his program so much that he transferred Bill to the Crime Stoppers program. It was a transfer that would allow the public to have greater access to Bill and his awareness programs for the community. He would miss working on child abuse investigations; however, he would enjoy the television exposure of the Crime Stoppers program and the closer availability the community would have in requesting his programs. The transfer was a great way to start 1985.

To this day, Bill can still recite the ending to the weekly crime of the week episode that aired every Tuesday night. "If you know the person or persons responsible for this crime, or any felony crime, call Crime Stoppers at 833-TIPS. You won't be asked for your name and you may earn up to a $1,000 cash reward." He enjoyed his time in the Crime Stoppers unit with his partner, Sgt. Don Geen, the sergeant who founded the Beaumont Crime Stoppers unit.

Unfortunately, time in the unit was short-lived. The finance director for the City of Beaumont had invested $20,000,000 with an investment firm in Florida. The returns on the money were almost too good to be true. Evidently, they were because the city lost that entire investment through a fraudulent scheme. It took years for the city to recover a portion of that money. In the meantime, the everyday regular people who worked for the city were the ones who lost the most. Departments throughout the city had to cut personnel. The police department had a union contract and the city could not fire any police officers nor cut their salaries. However, the city closed the city jail that housed prisoners on the basement level of the police station. The city also fired almost all civilian dispatchers, central records personnel, and other non-police support personnel in the department. Someone had to dispatch calls and answer the telephones. The only officers that were expendable were detectives. Suddenly, sergeants with many years of experience investigating crimes found themselves sitting at a desk in front of a dispatch terminal. Bill was one of them. For nineteen months, he was assigned as a midnight dispatcher along with several other sergeants.

As Bill began working his midnight shift tour of duty in dispatch, he wondered what would happen to his child abuse program and his children's safety program. To his surprise, people still called the police station for him to present his programs. He always made himself available, even if it meant a lack of sleep for him. He still took off, using his compensatory and vacation time, to present his presentations at conferences. He always made himself available to present programs to schools and civic organizations the entire time he worked the midnight shift.

Bill greatly missed investigating child abuse and sex crime incidents, but the programs were his. His off-duty time was his. His programs were in demand. God was keeping Bill busily at work!

The city slowly recovered most of the lost investment money. Departments slowly got their personnel back to full strength. Chief Swan moved on to another department. The city decided to not look outside the department again for a chief. This time, they hired from within. George Schuldt was the police department's next chief. He realized one great need that was lacking within the police department was a police-community relations department. Lt. Ed Woodsmall was transferred to oversee the new department. Sgt. Sonny Chambers and Officers Butch Pachall, Clara Boteler, and Gabe Duriso were assigned to the new unit. Within a few weeks, Bill was also assigned to be the second sergeant in the unit. The department's police-community relations unit opened even greater doors for Bill. His job was to develop a closer bond with the community than what the police department already had. His programs helped develop that closer bond. His awareness about child abuse and child safety not only continued throughout Southeast Texas but it allowed him to expand throughout the state presenting more workshops and presentations at conferences and seminars.

Things were jumping for Bill in the mid-1980s. He was on television a lot. His name was recognized throughout the community. His friend, Harold Engstrom, left the department and was appointed as Justice of the Peace to fill the position of Judge McNeil due to McNeil's retirement. The second justice of the peace for Jefferson County's Precinct 1, Judge McCasland also decided to retire at the end of his term. Bill thought long and hard about this position. He knew the law and had name recognition. After careful thought, he decided to do it. He put in his application, along with five other people, under the Democratic ticket. The primary election came in March 1986. Bill came in second place. The first-place contender was a Beaumont city councilwoman, Vi McGinnis. She did not receive fifty-plus percent of the votes, so a runoff election took place between her and Bill. The winner would be the new justice of the peace since no one ran for the position on the Republican ticket. Billboards were up. Yard signs were everywhere. Runoff Saturday came. Phone calls were made encouraging people to take time to vote. The day ended and the votes were counted. Bill lost. He was devastated. He knew he was qualified for the position. But he learned that in politics, that didn't matter. Vi McGinnis turned out to be a very good justice of the peace, a friend to law enforcement, and she held the position for twenty-four years. Bill could not understand why he did not win the race. He talked to God about it many times. Over the years, God's quiet, small voice answered Bill's question. Had he won the justice of the peace race, Bill quite possibly would have had to stop his programs. He would have never been in the police department's Sex Crimes Unit. He would have never been one of the investigators in Falyssa Van Winkle's murder. He would have never been the investigator in Tori Carpenter's case. He would have never written books about the two investigations. And, both books, which have sold thousands of copies throughout the world and increased awareness about child abuse, would not have made such a positive impact on thousands of lives. Bill was continuously learning how to listen to that quiet, small voice. God was definitely at work!

Bill's work with Crime Stoppers and his partner, Don Geen, lasted for about a year. When he was not getting ready to film his next 'Crime of the Week' segment, he was presenting programs to children in schools, civic organizations, churches, and basically, anywhere he was invited. In doing so, victims of crimes began to come forward. His programs brought people 'out of the closet,' especially crimes of a sexual nature. Children were making outcries of incest. Teenagers and adults were making outcries of sexual assault crimes. The department had an opening for lieutenant and gave the civil service examination for the position. Detective Sergeant Frank Coffin was one of the sergeants to take the exam. He was one of the two detectives assigned to the Sex Crimes Unit located within the Special Crimes Bureau of the department. Frank was promoted and assigned to be the lieutenant of the bureau he'd been working in. Now, an opening needed to be filled in the Sex Crimes Unit. Within days, Bill filled the opening. It was March 12, 1989. The unit had been investigating only adult sex crime incidents. However, with

LOOK OUT SATAN ~ GOD'S AT WORK!

Bill's expertise in investigating child physical and sexual incidents, the sexual incidents regarding children were moved from the juvenile detectives to the detectives in the Sex Crimes Unit.

Bill had a great partner in the Sex Crimes Unit. Faye Ford was the first female officer to be hired by the Beaumont Police Department. She was an exceptionally good officer, a particularly good partner, and was respected by everyone. It only took a few days for them to be swamped with incidents to investigate involving adult and child sex crime victims. Bill filmed his interviews with small children and presented those interviews to Ms. Mickey Mehaffy, an assistant district attorney at the Jefferson County District Attorney's office. Many of Bill's investigations also involved some very dedicated investigators with Child Protective Services. Many of these investigators were very good and the two agencies worked well together. But, there was one big problem. CPS investigators worked under the civil law of the Texas Family Code. Bill and other law enforcement investigators worked under the stricter criminal law under the Texas Penal Code. Most of the filmed interviews of children through CPS did not cover all of the criminal elements required by a Penal Code statute for law enforcement investigators to file a criminal charge(s) against someone. As the chief prosecutor, Mickey realized that something had to be done. She assembled a group of about eight to ten criminal and civil investigators from throughout the county. Bill was a member of her group. They met about once or twice a month to develop better ways to prepare prosecution for child abuse incidents.

Mickey heard about an entity called a children's advocacy center in Birmingham, Alabama. After visiting the site, she returned to Beaumont and contacted her group. Everyone agreed that one of these centers was needed for our children. There was only one like it in Texas, and it was in the panhandle. Our advocacy center would be the second one in Texas. An abandoned building was found. A non-profit organization agreed to financially help with the project. Renovations began.

As the project was nearing completion, Mickey left Beaumont on a Friday afternoon to meet her husband, Jim Mehaffy, in Austin. As she drove through a terrible thunderstorm, her vehicle hydroplaned and crashed into a tree. Mickey was killed instantly. As everyone grieved over the loss of this wonderful trailblazer, no one was about to see her project fall by the wayside.

The advocacy center was completed and opened in the summer of 1990. The Honorable Judge Jim Farris from Jefferson County was the keynote speaker of the day. He was one of the most prominent family court judges in Texas, one of the most sought-after public speakers in the nation, and was one of Bill's mentors. It was quite a day for the children of Southeast Texas.

The advocacy center has interviewed thousands of children since opening. These interviews are recorded. As a result, the child does not have to repeatedly tell their story of being abused and/or molested. Bill was also on the board of directors when the vote was passed to expand the advocacy center to include a counseling service for child victims and their families. This action allowed those victims and family members to go from being victims to survivors, and from survivors to overcomers. Bill served as a member of the advocacy center's board of directors for twenty years, the longest of any founding board member.

As Bill worked on one of his many investigations, Freddie Bobb, the Special Crimes Bureau secretary, called him. She said that a mother walked into their lobby with her eight-year-old daughter. Freddie told Bill the mother stated her daughter told her that her live-in boyfriend molested the child. Bill immediately stopped what he was doing and went to the lobby. He escorted the mother and her daughter to his office. As they sat, the mother stated she had been dating a man, Hulio, for about three months, and he moved into their home about six weeks earlier. The mother stated he exhibited an unusual interest in her daughter, but she thought nothing of it until her daughter began crying earlier in the day. When the mother asked her daughter what was wrong, the daughter said she didn't want Hulio coming into her room at night and touching her. Bill quickly made a police report and called the advocacy center for an appointment for the child to be given an opportunity to tell her story. The interview with the child was held two days later. The advocacy center's most seasoned forensic interviewer interviewed the child. For greater details, Bill called Hulio for an interview. The interview with Hulio was a couple of days later. A short time after giving Hulio the Miranda Warning, the suspect began admitting to sexually molesting the little girl. As Bill typed Hulio's confession statement, he was amazed at how matter-of-factly Hulio talked about going into the child's room at night and touching her. Bill was also amazed at how similar Hulio's confession matched the child's story in her taped interview. Bill's background check on Hulio prior to the interview also revealed that he had served seven years of a ten-year probation sentence for sexually molesting another eight-year-old child, seven years earlier. Hulio signed his written confession affidavit. Bill let Hulio leave his office knowing he would have Hulio in handcuffs in a day or two.

Hulio's first eight-year-old victim was now a fifteen-year-old teenager. Bill pulled her case file and reviewed its paperwork. It was an investigation that was assigned to another detective because Bill's caseload was so huge at the time. Bill called the teenager to his office and advised her of the new case. She stated she would be willing to testify at Hulio's probation revocation hearing if needed. Bill could tell that this teenager was still distraught and stressed by what this man did to her seven years earlier.

Bill spent the rest of the day typing his supplementary report and his probable cause affidavit on Hulio's investigation. He presented the case to the district attorney's office the next morning. The intake attorney issued a formal complaint against Hulio and Bill then went to Judge Engstrom's Justice of the Peace office. The judge issued a warrant for Hulio with a $100,000 bond. The bond didn't really matter because both men knew the probation office was going to place a 'hold' on Hulio due to molesting another child in violation of his probation. As Bill got back to his office, he called Hulio's probation officer. They set up an arrangement for Hulio to come to the probation office at 1:30 p.m. that day.

As Bill sat in the probation office parking lot that afternoon, he arranged with the dispatcher to have a patrol officer sitting in his patrol car in the police station parking lot a block away. Hulio was punctual. Bill saw his car as he parked in the parking lot and entered the courthouse annex building. Bill called the officer in the police parking lot and had him come to the courthouse annex parking lot. The officer was a field training officer and was accompanied by a rookie officer he was training. The three officers entered the building and walked to the probation office. The receptionist pointed the officers to Probation Officer Brown's office. As they entered Brown's office, Bill saw Hulio sitting in a chair to his left. He shook hands with the probation officer and then turned his attention to Hulio. "Hulio, it's a great day! In fact, I want you to do something for me," Bill stated in an almost arrogant tone. The rookie's eyes were wide open, wondering what this detective was doing. "I want you to inhale!" Bill exclaimed. Puzzled, Hulio looked at Bill and asked, "Huh?" "Breathe in, dang it!" Bill hollered. Hulio inhaled. "Now, breathe out!" Bill demanded. Hulio did so. With a grin, Bill told Hulio, "That was your last breath of free air! Stand up and put your hands on the wall you scumbag! I have a warrant for your arrest. You've molested your last child!" Bill instructed the rookie to frisk and handcuff their prisoner. It was the rookie's first arrest and one he would never forget.

Hulio's probation revocation hearing was several weeks later. The new victim testified against Hulio and then the fifteen-year-old girl testified. Bill was the last witness. The defense attorney had no witnesses in his client's defense. The judge pondered his decision for a few seconds, then had Hulio rise. As Hulio stood, the judge declared that he believed Hulio to be a sexual predator, especially to innocent eight-year-old girls. He also stated that he believed Hulio had done nothing more than manipulate the judicial system during his seven years on probation. The judge ended by sentencing Hulio to life in prison. Bill exited the courtroom, satisfied that he'd done his job. He prevented a manipulative sexual predator from molesting another child. The newer part of the courthouse has an oval opening in the center of the second and third floors so that the staircase and first floor can be viewed. Bill stood at the railing of the second-floor opening, talking to another officer. The courtroom began to empty. Bill saw the fifteen-year-old girl exit the courtroom and walk toward him. She was crying. She walked up to Bill, threw her arms around his neck, and cried. He held her until her tears subsided. Still holding him, she looked him in the eyes and made a statement Bill would never forget. "For the first time in seven years, I can finally sleep tonight." Her burden, her fear had been lifted.

Bill and the fifteen-year-old girl, Andrea, now a mature lady and one of the best bakers in Southeast Texas, are still good friends. In fact, she baked the cakes for Bill and Cheryl's wedding and they were 'sooooo' delicious! Thank you, Andrea!

"For he is God's servant for your good. But if you do wrong, (you should dread him and) be afraid, for he does not bear and wear the sword for nothing. He is God's servant to execute His wrath (punishment, vengeance) on the wrongdoer."
Romans 13:4 – The Amplified Bible

Bill's yard poster when he campaigned for Justice of the Peace in 1986.

Photo of a 'Cop Collectibles' card
Bill autographed to Andrea.

Chapter Ten

True Crime Books

"Oh, that my words were now written! Oh, that they were inscribed in a book." Job 19:23 – New American Standard Bible

The year 1990 was quite busy. Requests for Bill's programs were steadily increasing. As the programs increased awareness throughout Southeast Texas, more validated child abuse and sex crime incidents were coming to light. Renovations on the old building that would soon house the second children's advocacy center in the State of Texas was drawing closer to completion.

The phone rang at Bill's home. It was Sunday, October 7, 1990, 10:00 a.m. When he answered, Bill recognized the voice of his friend, Frank Coffin, and also his lieutenant in charge of the Special Crimes Bureau. He quickly asked Bill if he had heard about the kidnapping and murder of a ten-year-old little girl the day before. Bill had not watched the news on Saturday and told Frank, "No." Frank explained that a little girl had been kidnapped from Larry's Antique Mall and Flea Market. He continued, telling Bill the girl's body was found under the Big Cow Creek Bridge in southern Newton County, about sixty miles north of Beaumont. Bill was glad to help but was a little confused. Why was he getting this phone call? He was not a 'homicide' detective. He was a 'sex crimes' detective. And then Frank lowered the boom. The autopsy had just been completed, Frank told Bill. This precious, innocent little girl had been viciously raped and then strangled to death. "I'll be right there," Bill told his friend. He was about to become involved in an investigation that would change his life.

Bill arrived at the Detective Division of the Beaumont Police Department a few minutes later. Another friend, Sgt. Bill Tatum, was also in the detective assembly room. Tatum was in charge of the Identification and Forensics Crimes Unit of the police department. A video had been made of the crime scene under the bridge the day before and all of the detectives present watched it. Frank advised both Bills they needed to get up to the bridge where the girl was found. Frank said that all of the homicide detectives were at the trade show searching for clues to determine who committed this vicious, despicable crime and he needed the two Bills to find some clue under the bridge that would help solve the case.

Before arriving at the bridge, their dispatcher advised the two detectives to meet the Newton County Sheriff at the Kirbyville Police Department. Tatum and Davis were advised that officers from the Kirbyville Police Department had two men detained that could be suspects in the little girl's murder. As they arrived, they introduced themselves to Wayne Powell, the Newton County sheriff. Both men who were detained had good alibis and did not appear to be the person or persons they were looking for in Falyssa Van Winkle's murder. They were released.

The Big Cow Creek Bridge was only eight miles away. Tatum, Davis, and Sheriff Powell headed to the bridge. Upon arrival, the two detectives got busy documenting everything they saw. It didn't take long to realize it may be October, but it felt more like an August afternoon as both detectives were sweating profusely. It was only 98 degrees that afternoon. Tatum photographed everything he saw under the bridge, took soil samples, and collected other forensic items for documentation. Bill got pen and paper and began sketching the underside of the bridge. He also took measurements tying the mud puddle where Falyssa was found to bridge pillars and the bridge to Hwy. 87, which was one-fourth of a mile away. They finished their work at approximately 5:30 p.m. and called the police station. Coffin advised them to stay with the sheriff for now. The homicide detectives at the trade show grounds had not come up with any leads on a suspect. Everyone was hoping a suspect would surface with the detectives in Newton County.

Tatum and Davis parked their detective cars at a convenience store, went inside, and got something to eat. After renewing their energy with some hot dogs, they got into the sheriff's car. There was no need for them to caravan throughout Newton County. Phone calls with possible leads on the murder of Falyssa came into the sheriff's dispatch office throughout the evening. Several calls were of the nature that, "Y'all need to check out this guy living two doors down," (or information to that effect). The caller would state, "He moved into that house six months ago and he just looks like a murderer." But one call came into the dispatcher's office around 8:00 p.m. The caller stated that three young men were almost run over by a guy driving a white van with a red bird painted on the rear of the vehicle. The caller also stated the van came from under the bridge at a high rate of speed, almost striking the vehicle occupied by the young men. The dispatcher conveyed the information of the phone call via the police radio, and the details of the call piqued the interest of the three law enforcement officers.

Sheriff Powell began driving toward the address he was given. It was pitch-black dark. The three law enforcement officers were driving down the dirt road to the address they were given when they noticed a vehicle driving toward them. The sheriff slowed his vehicle to a stop. As the oncoming vehicle approached them, the sheriff rolled his window down. He began waving his arm slowly for the vehicle to stop. It did. The vehicle was occupied by three young black males. The sheriff identified himself and the two detectives. He told the young men he was looking for a couple of young men, possibly brothers, that lived on that road, and who were almost run over by a van coming from under the Big Cow Creek Bridge earlier that day. He further advised the young men that the brothers they were looking for may be key witnesses in identifying the murderer of the ten-year-old little girl found dead under that bridge. Two of the three young men in the vehicle began to yell excitedly that they were the brothers he was looking for. They quickly exited their vehicle. The officers did the same. All six men were now standing in the middle of the dirt road talking to each other. The brothers quickly told the law enforcement officers how they were with a deaf cousin and were driving over the bridge when a big white van with a red bird painted on it came 'flying' from under the bridge. The big van turned right in front of them and the brother who was driving had to slam on his vehicle's brakes to keep from having a bad collision with the van. The officers advised the brothers they needed to follow them to the Beaumont Police Department to give sworn statements. One of the brothers advised the officers he was in the U.S. Navy and they were en route to return him to the Naval Air Station outside Corpus Christi where he was stationed and he had to be there by 6:00 a.m. or he would be AWOL (Absent Without Official Leave). Sheriff Powell took the name and phone number of the young man's commanding officer and told him not to worry. He told the young man that he was a crucial witness in a capital murder investigation and his sworn statement was vital. The three young men returned to their vehicle and drove home to inform their mother of what had just occurred.

Before following the young men to their home, the three experienced law enforcement officers continued to stand in the road looking at each other in amazement. What were the odds that three young black men would stop their vehicle on a dark dirt road for three older white men – and then talk to them? What were the odds that the officers would be traveling on the same dirt road at the same time their potential key witnesses would be traveling in the opposite direction – and then stop and talk to them? What if the three young black men would have kept driving, instead of slowing and stopping for someone 'flagging' them down? For the investigators, their key witnesses would have been gone. But, the vehicle stopped. The vehicle contained the brothers the officers were looking for. Sheriff Powell, Tatum, and Davis were beyond excited. They had just witnessed/experienced Divine Intervention in their investigation!!

Through the collaborative effort of several deputies from the Orange County Sheriff's Department, the Newton County Sheriff's Department, the Beaumont Police Department, and members of the Jefferson County District Attorney's Office, James Rexford Powell was arrested for Capital Murder seven hours later.

May 1991 was quite busy at the Newton County Courthouse with jury selection. Twelve people from over 300 potential jurors were finally selected. District Judge Joe Bob Golden selected Tuesday, the day after Memorial Day weekend, to begin testimony. As the day began, Jefferson County Assistant District Attorney Paul McWilliams gave his opening statement and began calling witnesses. Noon approached and Judge Golden called for a recess. McWilliams approached Davis and made a special request. Dr. Molina, the pathologist who had conducted the autopsy on Falyssa, was going to be the first witness after lunch and Paul needed to be sure the doctor was at the courthouse at 1:30 p.m. Bill promised Paul the doctor would be there on time.

Bill grabbed a quick cheeseburger, fries, and a drink as he drove through Beaumont. He pulled into the parking lot of Dr. Molina's medical office in Nederland, Texas. He identified himself to the receptionist and told her why he was there. She advised him to have a seat in the lobby and she would let the doctor know he was there. It was 11:45 a.m. At 12:00 p.m. Bill inquired how much longer the doctor would be. After all, it was seventy miles from Nederland to Newton and Bill promised Paul he would have the doctor at the courthouse at 1:30 p.m. It would take over an hour to drive that route due to traffic. The receptionist responded that the doctor was still seeing patients and he would be available as soon as possible. Bill asked the receptionist again at 12:15 p.m. if the doctor was close to being ready. He was getting irritated, and so was she. At 12:30 p.m., a patient opened the entrance/exit door to leave the examination room area of the facility. Bill entered the door and saw the doctor in the hallway. He was about to enter another exam room to see another patient. Bill walked up to the doctor and identified himself. The doctor advised Bill that he would be ready to go with him when he finished seeing his patients. Bill advised the doctor that he was leaving with him right then so they could arrive on time, voluntarily, or in handcuffs. Either way, they were not going to be late and upset a district judge and possibly cause a mistrial in a capital murder case. They stared at each other for a few seconds. The doctor quietly advised his nurse to reschedule his remaining patients. He walked with Bill to the detective's car. As they sat inside the car, Bill handed the doctor his notes surrounding the investigation. It was over thirty typewritten pages. He told the doctor not to look up from reading. It was 12:40 p.m. Bill had fifty minutes to travel seventy miles in congested traffic.

As Bill drove at almost lightning speed, Dr. Molina continued to read Bill's notes. He seemed to be engrossed in them. He was surprised that Bill drove as fast as he did as they entered the city limits of Newton. It was fast. Bill drove the car into a parking space at the Newton County Courthouse. It was exactly 1:30 p.m. Bill had gotten the doctor to the courthouse to testify on time. As the men were exiting the car, the doctor handed Bill's notes back to him, looked him in the eyes, and said, "You need to write a book about this case." They hurried inside the courthouse to the courtroom where everyone was waiting for them. Dr. Molina began his testimony.

As Dr. Molina ended his testimony, Bill escorted the doctor back to his detective car and drove him back to his office at a much slower speed than the previous trip. They didn't talk a lot, but Bill did ask the doctor a few questions about his statement about possibly writing a book. They arrived at the doctor's office and Bill thanked him for his testimony. The doctor entered his office and Bill drove away.

That night, Bill had a hard time falling asleep. That quiet, small voice kept talking to Bill. God was at work in this investigation and trial (as He is in all investigations and trials). Bill witnessed miracles in this investigation unlike anything he had ever seen.

The trial ended a few days later. Rex Powell was found guilty of capital murder by the jury in only forty-five minutes. After the punishment testimony and final arguments, the jury handed Rex his punishment. He received the death penalty in less than thirty-five minutes. The U.S. Supreme Court reinstated the death penalty in 1976. Through the years, Bill has tried to find another case where the defendant was found guilty of capital murder and sentenced to death more quickly than Rex Powell. To date, he has found no one.

As the days, weeks, and months went by after Rex's trial, that quiet, small voice would not go away. It kept urging Bill to write the book about Falyssa. A criminal justice professor at Lamar University asked Bill to speak to his students about child abuse awareness. As requested, Bill spoke to the students. After the class, Bill told the professor he was thinking about writing a book about Falyssa's murder. The professor was aware of the case and the trial due to all of the news publicity. "I don't know how to write a book," Bill told the professor. "Just write it," the professor responded. Bill never talked to the professor again, but he never forgot his advice.

Bill worked an off-duty extra job every Monday night. His job was to escort ladies getting off work from their telecommunications job every thirty minutes from the building to their vehicles. That quiet, small voice kept talking. Bill finally decided to see if he could actually write a book. He carried a yellow pad and his notes with him one night to the extra job. He was at the job from 6:00 p.m. to 2:15 a.m. Sometimes he had thirty minutes to an hour between shifts of ladies getting off work with nothing to do. He started writing. As he wrote, he prayed, "Lord, help me. I don't know what I'm doing. But, You do. Please guide me. Amen."

Bill worked on the book's manuscript every Monday night. Many times during the week, Bill would go to various people who were involved in the investigation and trial to be sure all of the facts were correct. Many people thought his project was a great idea. Falyssa's mom loved the idea. She told Bill on one occasion, "Please don't let my daughter's memory die." But some of Bill's colleagues heckled him. Some of them laughed at Bill telling him he was "stupid for wasting his time." One colleague told Bill, "You know you can't publish a book," and laughed at him. But, that quiet, small voice kept telling Bill, "Don't stop!"

After 1-1/2 years, Bill finally finished his manuscript. Now, he needed a publisher. Bill had no idea where to go. He looked inside books at bookstores and wrote down the names and addresses of publishing companies. Most of them were in New York City. Over the next 5-1/2 years he wrote to many of them and sent a copy of his manuscript with each letter. Many of the companies kept his manuscript for up to three months before returning it to Bill. Some of the companies kept the manuscript and sent a letter saying they were not interested in publishing his book. One editor sent Bill a letter. He stated the "bad guy didn't kill enough people to interest him." How callous.

As the years went by, Bill became discouraged. He felt his colleagues were right. He had wasted thousands of hours of his time writing a manuscript that would never become a book. But, that quiet, small voice kept saying, "Don't stop."

Bill enjoyed investigating sex crime incidents and saving children's and rape victims' lives. One day he received a phone call from a friend and colleague, Major Ben Moore, from the Hardin County Sheriff's Department. They exchanged pleasantries for a few minutes and then Ben got to the reason for his call. He had been investigating a case where a father allegedly sexually molested his daughter. He continued by stating that this man allegedly began the molestation when the daughter was four-years-old and ended when the child's mother walked into their home a few nights earlier and caught him. Ben told Bill the child had allegedly been molested by the father for over seven years and she was now eleven-years-old. Ben continued by saying that he took the child to the children's advocacy center for an interview, and a judge issued a warrant on the man for Aggravated Sexual Assault of a Child. Ben continued by saying the guy was a contractor, had money, and bonded out of the Hardin County jail in about two hours. Bill was intrigued by Ben's story but still did not understand why Ben was calling him about this investigation. And then, Ben dropped the bomb. He told Bill this father did not start molesting his daughter in Hardin County. Ben said, "Bill, he started molesting her in your town. You need to take over this investigation." Ben further explained that the family lived in a residential neighborhood in Beaumont before moving to one-hundred acres of land at the dead end of a road in a wooded area northwest of Lumberton. The two investigators ended their conversation with Bill making an appointment to meet with Ben the next day to begin the process of taking over the investigation. Bill looked at his stack of folders, each an investigation for him to solve. There were not enough hours in the day to investigate the cases he already had. Now, he was about to add another case to the already overwhelming pile.

After meeting with Ben and taking over the investigation, Bill spent hours reviewing the paperwork of the sheriff's department investigation and the videotape of the child's interview at the children's advocacy center. It was obvious this eleven-year-old child was not an average eleven-year-old child. From watching the advocacy center interview, Bill could see that the child was extremely intelligent. He called the child's mother, Martha, and set up a time for him to begin her daughter's investigation with an interview and sworn affidavit the next morning.

The next morning, Bill visited with Martha, her daughter, Tori, and Crystal Roosevelt, a representative from the victim's advocacy department of the district attorney's office. After explaining how he would conduct the interview with Tori, Bill asked Martha to wait in the lobby. Bill had learned many years earlier that parents should NEVER be in a room where a child is interviewed. One of the main reasons for this procedure is that children love their parents and do not want to hurt them. Many times a child will withhold information because it might hurt their parents' feelings if the parent is in the interview room with them. Another reason is that parents tend to be emotional, which also causes children to withhold information. Crystal's job was simple. She was there to hold Tori's hand and be supportive to her as she told her story to Bill.

Bill listened as Tori began telling her story. He was amazed at the details she remembered and conveyed to him. There was no way this eleven-year-old girl was making up the details she was telling him as they talked. Bill had learned and developed a philosophy many years earlier – Children deserve the right to be HEARD, and Children deserve the right to be BELIEVED! Bill was not pulling information from Tori. It was obvious she had found someone who would listen to her and believe her. Three days later, sixteen hours of interviewing, and twelve single-space, typewritten, legal-size affidavit pages later, Tori's story was documented. Her interview was the longest interview Bill conducted with any victim and her affidavit was the longest affidavit he took from anyone.

Bill worked feverishly for days corroborating Tori's story. Martha called Bill daily and told him of incidents where Steve, her husband, and Bill's suspect, was stalking and tormenting her and the children. He had to protect them. One of the people Bill interviewed was Steve's sister, June. She was worried for the safety of Martha, Tori, and Luke. So, she allowed them to stay for several days in her home for protection. Bill visited Martha and the children at June's home on several occasions as he worked to develop his probable cause to arrest Steve. June was a civil attorney with a law office in Beaumont. During one of their conversations, June told Bill that her undergraduate degree was in Political Science, and her minor was in English. Their conversation continued with Bill telling her about writing the manuscript to a true crime story about a ten-year- old little girl who was kidnapped, raped, and murdered from a local trade show. June remembered the newspaper and television stories about the tragedy. Bill told her about trying to get the manuscript published for 5-1/2 years with no luck. She told Bill that she would love to read his manuscript. So, the next day, Bill brought the manuscript to her.

Tori's investigation became more and more complex. Bill coordinated with the Hardin County Sheriff's Department to carry out a search warrant at Steve's house one afternoon. Bill was hurriedly trying to execute the search warrant early that day because it was his birthday and he wanted to celebrate it with his family. But, Steve would have none of that. As sheriff's deputies surrounded his house that afternoon waiting for Bill to arrive with the search warrant, they heard a gunshot from within the residence. Checking on Steve, the deputies discovered that he shot himself in the upper chest. He was rushed to a hospital. It was discovered a short time later that his wound was not life-threatening. From this incident, Bill began to learn that Steve was a master manipulator, as many sexual predators are. The shooting incident was Steve's way of not going to jail that day. Bill's wife and son celebrated his birthday without him.

Bill visited with Martha, the children, and June shortly after the shooting incident. He learned that Steve called Martha that day and was trying to convince her to get Tori to change her story and tell Bill that her story was all a lie. When Martha said she believed her daughter one-hundred percent, she heard him shoot himself. Bill assured Martha that Steve would make a full recovery and he would be arrested. Before leaving the residence, June told Bill she read his manuscript and loved it. She asked if he ever thought of self-publishing his book. He had heard of self-publishing, but never checked into it. June explained the issue to him. It sounded interesting, but Bill told June that self-publishing obviously took money and he did not have it. "I'll do it," she said. "Do what?" Bill asked. "I'll provide the money," June told Bill. He was trying to comprehend what she was saying. She explained her belief that Falyssa's story needed to be told. She said she believed that telling Falyssa's story would save the lives of many children and she was willing to 'front' the money to make it happen. She also committed her paralegal secretary as an editor for the manuscript and making the manuscript 'print ready.'

LOOK OUT SATAN ~ GOD'S AT WORK!

Bill left June's house a few minutes later, still trying to soak in what had just happened. He got in his detective car and drove a couple of blocks and parked next to the curb. God's quiet voice wasn't quiet. God was yelling in Bill's ears, "It's time! It's here!" As Bill wiped away tears of joy, he realized he had worked seven years trying to get Falyssa's story told. And now, it was here. Wait, Bill thought – seven years! And then God shared with Bill one of His favorite numbers – Seven! God created the week to be seven days. He created the heavens and the earth in six days and then He rested on the seventh. Bill thought, 'Wow! The number 'Seven' is God's perfect number!' Bill worked seven years trying to get his book published, and now it was about to become reality. The determination he learned and developed through his surgeries and year of rehabilitation prepared him to deal with all the obstacles he encountered and overcame to tell Falyssa's story.

The next few weeks were crazy. Bill finally put Steve in jail. Four days later, another seasoned investigator and Bill went to a mountaintop ranch outside of Alpine, Texas to complete Tori's investigation. Steve took his family to this ranch two months earlier declaring that he and his family would be living on that ranch for at least four to five years while he built a hunting lodge and renovated the ranch house for the multi-millionaire rancher. Since Martha home-schooled the children, they were the perfect family to live there on that ranch (according to Steve) which was at 6,000 feet in elevation, for that long period of time. Tori explained to Bill in her interview that her father sexually molested her while they were on top of that mountain. From Tori's description, Bill and his investigator friend, Rick, immediately found the location Tori described where the molestation took place. What surprised the two investigators was that they found evidence of the two-month-old molestation in a semi-open area to the elements. Bill collected unique evidence that he had never seen in thousands of investigations. Tori's case was unique and easily the second most complex case he ever investigated.

Bill contacted a friend who owned a local printing company. They were excited to help Bill's dream become a reality. Thanks to June's financial support, Bill's first order of books was 10,000 copies. The owner of the trade show, Larry, called Bill and wanted the book to debut at the trade show as a tribute to Falyssa. This was very important to Larry because his granddaughter was walking around the trade show grounds with Falyssa the Saturday morning she was kidnapped. Larry could hardly talk about Falyssa's incident without having tears in his eyes, knowing that Rex Powell could have easily kidnapped his own granddaughter instead of Falyssa. Saturday, December 12, 1998, was selected as the day of the trade show weekend for the book to be introduced to the world.

October 1998 was another turning point in Bill's life. A local chamber of commerce asked Bill to present several television public service announcements about child abuse awareness and child safety through a grant this chamber received. As the public service announcements hit the airwaves, they began receiving great reviews. Also in that month, Bill was asked to be a presenter at a state conference in Corpus Christi. He took a couple of compensatory days and left on Thursday for the conference. That evening, Bill had the great honor of having dinner with the Honorable Jim Farris. Judge Farris was the final speaker at the conference.

Bill returned home on Saturday evening after the conference ended and immediately began preparing for a busy week ahead. He was scheduled to present his week-long child abuse seminar at the regional police academy to a room full of law enforcement officers that upcoming week.

Bill got up extra early that Monday morning. He arrived at his office about 7:00 a.m. He reviewed phone messages received on Thursday and Friday and checked on some of his investigations before leaving for the police academy. Bill's immediate boss surprised him as he walked through Bill's office door and sat down. The boss usually didn't get to work that early. He asked Bill how the

LOOK OUT SATAN ~ GOD'S AT WORK!

conference was and Bill told him about Judge Farris being a keynote speaker and that the conference was great. His boss then told him that a decision had been made while he was gone. The boss told Bill he was unanimously chosen to fill the vacancy in the patrol division as a sergeant on day shift. "What?" Bill yelled at his boss. "What have I done wrong to deserve this?" He was in shock. The types of crimes he investigated was his passion. Suddenly, while he was out of town promoting child abuse awareness and indirectly promoting the Beaumont Police Department, his professional rug had been jerked out from under him. He had been stabbed in the back while out of town. His boss assured him that he had done nothing wrong, but the decision was final. Bill jumped out of his chair and began yelling at his boss, who quickly ran from Bill's office (In fear? Who knows.) Bill was completely blindsided and devastated. He was crushed. He wiped away his tears and left for the police academy. He had a class to teach. The information he could share with the officers of that class may save a child's life.

As Bill drove to the police academy, he called his pastor, Ralph. Bill was crushed by his transfer. He desperately needed to talk to someone. Ralph realized that the situation was serious and his friend was going to need more counseling than a conversation during a quick phone call. He suggested that he and Bill meet during Bill's lunch hour and talk. Bill chose the parking lot of a local fast-food restaurant on College St. in Beaumont as the place to meet with Ralph. Somehow, with God's help, Bill managed to present his morning lecture to the officers without breaking down and crying.

Bill dismissed the class for lunch early. He arrived at the restaurant parking lot, and his friend and pastor was there waiting on him. Ralph got into the passenger side of Bill's detective car. Bill explained to Ralph what happened with him and his boss that morning. He explained that the only feasible explanation he could think of for the transfer was jealousy. Bill explained there was jealousy over the publicity of his book, the public service announcements he starred in on television, and his increasing number of programs. Ralph stated to Bill that he (Bill) was the only person he knew that could go into a school and talk about God and sex and get paid for it.

They both grinned, and then Ralph quietly asked Bill about how many programs he was presenting per year. Bill answered, "I don't really know – about fifty or sixty per year." "You have a lot of cases to investigate, don't you?" Ralph asked. "Yes, my partners and I are so overloaded, we need another investigator," Bill answered. "What if this transfer frees you up to present eighty or maybe a hundred or more presentations per year?" Ralph asked. "You're crazy. That'll never happen!" Bill yelled. "But what if it does?" Ralph asked. "How many more lives can you save with your programs than solving your cases!" Ralph said, rather than asking. He made his point. Ralph made another statement. He told Bill to start praying for his boss and at least one other person who had probably been involved in this decision to transfer him. "Like hell I will!" Bill yelled. Ralph asked Bill if he thought those who made the transfer decision were going to lose sleep over the decision. Bill got quiet. Ralph suggested to Bill that he give his burden to God, to throw it at God's feet and let Him handle it. Still mad and upset, Bill said he would pray for them, with his teeth gritted. Ralph grinned and got out of the car. He told Bill, "Grit your teeth if you want, but let Him deal with it. That's His job," and he closed the door. Bill had to hurry. It was time to start the afternoon session of his child abuse awareness class. It was time to save some lives.

Within two years, Bill was traveling and presenting his programs to over a hundred locations per year throughout the United States and internationally. He realized that this number of programs would not have been possible if he was still investigating child abuse and sexual incidents. And, some really bad things happened to those involved with Bill's transfer. As those things happened, Bill realized God's justice was far above anything he imagined would ever happen to those people. Bill realized that when people do bad things to you, give it to God. That's His job. Let Him handle it, not you. Bill also learned to give God thanks in all things.

The media did a great job publicizing the debut of Bill's book. As Bill arrived at the trade show, he was amazed at the long line of people waiting to purchase an autographed copy of the book. It was quite a busy day and many books were autographed. But, that was just the beginning. More than 50,000 copies later, this book continues to be a big seller. The colleagues who laughed at Bill and the thought of him having a book published, were buying his book and asking him to autograph it for them. In the first paragraph of the book's acknowledgments, Bill thanked God for choosing him to write the book and for giving him the fortitude and perseverance to complete the task. That God-given fortitude and perseverance to never give up took him back to January 7, 1984, at 7:05 a.m.

The day for Tori's trial was quickly approaching. Three days prior to the beginning of the trial, Crystal, the victim's advocate, met Tori, her brother Luke, and Martha in the courthouse lobby. She escorted them to a courtroom similar to where Steve's trial would be held. The courtroom was vacant that afternoon due to a trial being settled out of court. Tori was the prosecution's star witness. She was quite nervous as any witness would be, especially being only twelve years old. There was no DNA evidence. Martha caught Steve coming out of the bathroom occupied by Tori, but hadn't caught him in the actual act of sexually molesting their daughter. It was basically their word against Steve's word. Crystal had Tori sit in the witness chair and look out over the courtroom. Crystal sat in one of the front-row seats. Crystal identified this is where she would be sitting as Tori testified, and Tori could look at her when she gave her answers. This simple act would help Tori as she testified.

Monday came and Judge Barnes read his docket for the week. Tori's case was number five on the docket. Prior cases took up the week. Her case was re-set several weeks later. They were all disappointed.

BILL DAVIS

Tori's second trial setting was number four on the docket that Monday. Tori, her mom, and her brother were all excited that they would be going to trial that week. Another trial took up the week and their case was re-set again. They were now beginning to realize that the judicial system is like a roller coaster ride – high with anticipation one minute, only to be at a low with disappointment the next minute.

Tori's trial was now number three on the judge's docket and the three witnesses were sure their case would go to trial. Each of them had gone over their testimony countless times in their mind. They were ready. As Judge Barnes read the docket, only two cases were ahead of them. Surely, they would begin their trial this week. The second case on the docket took all week to reach a verdict. Their case was re-set again. Tori was devastated. Martha was angry. She called Bill, the only person who had not let her down. Bill answered his phone and recognized Martha's voice. He immediately heard the anger and frustration in her voice. He was not aware that Tori's case was being re-set for the fourth time. He stopped what he was doing and listened. After she finished venting her frustrations, he asked her if he could tell her a story and she agreed to listen.

Bill began telling her about a young lady named Summer, who attended his church. Summer was sexually molested by her stepfather from the age of eleven to nineteen years old. He got her pregnant when she was seventeen years old. Bill continued Summer's storytelling to Martha that Summer's mother sided with her husband even though she was aware he got her daughter pregnant. He also told Martha that Summer's case was investigated and the stepfather was jailed. But, the stepfather's attorney got his trial continued more than fifteen times with the hope that Summer would get so angry at the judicial system that she would throw her hands in the air and give up. Bill told Martha that on several occasions Summer saw him as he greeted people at the main entrance of their church. Her three-year-old daughter, Gracie, always saw Mr. Bill at the church entrance and ran to give him a hug. Bill always saw

Gracie running and always knelt to receive a big hug as he held the door open for her to enter. As the church service began, Summer met Bill in the church foyer after taking Gracie to 'children's church' on several occasions. She told him that she was dropping charges against her stepfather the next day because her case had been re-set for the 'umpteenth' time. Every time this happened, Bill convinced Summer to not drop the charges. Ultimately, Summer's stepfather received two twenty-five year prison sentences. The judge ordered the sentences to run back-to-back for a total of fifty years. Bill told Martha, that Summer's stepfather would probably die in prison.

And, Summer's mother was supportive of him, not her daughter. As Bill finished Summer's story, Martha took a deep breath and told Bill no matter how many times Steve's attorney had his trial re-set, they would be ready. She thanked him for his time and the call ended. Bill hung up his phone and shook his head at how the 'system' victimizes the victim over and over.

Summer kept in touch with Bill throughout the years. Her biological father lives in another state and rarely communicates with her. Her biological mother had no communication with her from the time of her stepfather's arrest through the trial and even after he was sent to prison. Her mother remained supportive of him until her death in 2021. He is still in prison.

Summer called Bill and Cheryl in 2019 and told them her family made a command decision. She declared that they were now HER adopted parents and they now had three new grandchildren. The Bible stresses that adoption is closer than biological. One is a choice. The other is not. Bill and Cheryl are very close to Dusty and his family. They are also very close to Summer and her family. Cheryl was also adopted. She thanks God every day for her adoption. She is forever grateful for the love of both of her families. Her life is greatly enriched by the positive choices made on her behalf. "Thank you, Lord! What a wonderful life!"

Steve's trial was finally here. Steve's attorney invoked 'the rule' which meant no witness could hear another witness's testimony. All witnesses, except Tori, left the courtroom. Bill could not listen to her testimony, but he took one last look inside the courtroom as he went through the exit door. He saw Tori as she took her seat in the witness chair. She was so small in such a big chair. He could barely see her head over the rail that was around the witness chair. It was so disgusting to think that her father would put her through the horrible rigors of testifying. Tori never refused to answer any question asked of her by Randy, the prosecuting attorney, or Stewart, her father's defense attorney, with her father, her molester, sitting twenty feet away. Bill took one last look at Tori as the courtroom door closed behind him. He had just seen a REAL hero!

Barbara Harrison, the sexual assault nurse examiner, who conducted the forensic sexual exam on Tori, was the next witness, followed by Bill testifying. Randy called two more witnesses, then rested the state's case. It was Stewart's turn. He called his one witness – Steve. An old cliché came to Bill's mind, "You can't fix stupid." Steve testified on his own behalf.

As Stewart ended the defense's case and the attorneys gave their final arguments, the jury was escorted to the jury room to deliberate Steve's guilt or innocence. It didn't take them long, three hours-and-fifty-eight minutes – guilty. Martha, Tori, and Luke were all relieved. The wait had been worthwhile.

The punishment of Steve's trial began that afternoon. Several witnesses were called. The attorneys gave their final arguments. The jurors were escorted to the jury room. It was 4:00 p.m. Everyone kept their seats. Thirty-eight minutes later, Judge Barnes announced, "The jury has reached a decision." Everyone held their breath as the twelve men and women were escorted back to the jury box. Bill sat on the courtroom bench holding Martha's hand on one side and Tori's hand on the other side. The jury foreman announced that a decision had been reached. Steve received seventy-five years in the Texas penitentiary system for his atrocious crimes.

LOOK OUT SATAN ~ GOD'S AT WORK!

Bill exited the courtroom ahead of everyone else. As he visited with another officer, Tori exited the courtroom with her mother and brother. She walked up to Bill. He ended his conversation with the officer and turned his attention to the precious twelve-year-old child at his side. He asked her if she was okay and she told him, "Yes." She then asked him, "Mister Bill, you wrote a book, didn't you?" She was aware that her aunt had helped Bill publish his book. He responded by answering her question in the affirmative. He reminded her that she had seen copies of his book. Tori then looked Bill directly in his eyes and made a profound statement, "Well then, maybe if you wrote another book and told my story, maybe you and me could save some lives!" Bill was speechless. God's quiet, small voice had spoken to Bill again, through the voice of a sweet, innocent twelve-year-old child. Bill told her he would see what he could do. Tori then left with her mother and brother to begin another chapter in their lives.

God's quiet, small voice through Tori would not go away. Bill began to write once again. Many times, he would work on the manuscript of Tori's story and then go for months without typing a word. Bill worked on the manuscript for several years and still did not have a title. He was driving home one evening after working on the manuscript all day. As he drove westbound on College St. in Beaumont, Bill began talking to God and venting his frustrations of not being able to think of a title. BAM! It was as if God hit him in the head with a 2x4 board: *Imperfect Love ~ Imperfect Justice*. That was it! God gave Bill the perfect title. Her father's love had been horrible. And no matter how stiff her father's punishment was, nothing could erase the memory of his sexual and horrible deeds. Twelve years after Tori asked Bill to tell her story, his second true crime book was published.

Many women have approached Bill and asked what his second book was about. As he gave a synopsis of the book, many have looked at him and said he was telling their story, only the names, dates, and places are different. He has given many ladies a tissue as they tell him their story. Bill always tells them he wishes he could have had the opportunity to investigate their abuse and seek justice for them. He also tells them he hopes they have been successful in going from being a victim, to being a survivor, and becoming an overcomer. Men have also told Bill his book is telling their story, too, with different names, dates, places, and sex. May God Bless them all!

Bill's two true crime books continue to sell thousands of copies throughout the world. One of Bill's greatest honors is to have the opportunity to personally autograph his books to someone.

For more awesome, riveting details, read Bill's true crime books, *So Innocent, Yet So Dead*, and *Imperfect Love ~ Imperfect Justice*! Call Bill to get his books.

Summer

Bill and his Granddaughter, Gracie

Bill and Granddaughter, Lillian, who is one of his many 'Junior Officers.'

Chapter Eleven

More Programs

"And we know that all things work together for good to them that love God, to them who are called according to His purpose." Romans 8:28 – King James Version

Bill's involvement with the advocacy center introduced him to a lady who was also instrumental with the center. As she found out about Bill's child abuse seminar and his children's safety program, she mentioned to him that he was leaving out an entire group in our population – TEENAGERS. A seed was planted. That quiet, small voice started speaking to Bill again. He realized he would need to create a program that would be educational for teenagers and at the same time be entertaining and memorable. Suddenly, that quiet, small voice gave him one word – SEX! Bill got busy investing hundreds of hours of his time and money to develop another program. As Bill began presenting his new program to teenage audiences, one of his first statements to the audience is that, "I think SEX is one of the greatest things God ever created and personally, I love it." That statement has teenagers laughing and giving Bill one-hundred percent of their attention. Bill continues on by telling teenagers, "But, I think sex should be between a man and a woman, happily married." Through the years, this statement has become socially incorrect and Bill has been called out for not being socially correct. His response is always that he will be glad to change his statement as soon as God changes his view on the issue. Another Biblical statement that Bill makes in his presentation is promoting virginity and telling teenagers to be proud of their virginity until marriage, and not be ashamed of it. (Another socially incorrect statement, but correct according to God's

Holy Word.)

The first opportunity to present this new program came on February 4, 1991, from a teacher at Westbrook High School. Bill presented it under the title of "Date Rape." He kept this title for his teenager's program for five years. He was constantly adding new slides to the presentation. He added a new section to the program, dealing not with criminal law and sex, but civil law as it deals with sex. Most girls in his audiences believe that if they get pregnant, they only have two options – keep the baby or abortion. Bill educates girls by adding two more options – adoption and the Texas 'Baby Moses' law. He shows the audience a photo of his own son, Dusty's first baby picture, and then a photo of Dusty, now a grown man, and he and Bill standing side by side. He explains to the group that he thanks God every day for the woman who gave birth to his son and chose the second "A" word, adoption, instead of the first "A" word, abortion.

Bill also added a topic to the civil law section about child support. Then, he came up with a novel idea. He would get a real boyfriend/girlfriend couple from the audience to volunteer and help him with a skit. The boy would stand by a large dry-erase board. The girl sits on the stage or in a chair and holds a baby doll that Bill brings especially for the program. The scenario for the skit is that the couple went to a secluded place and had a few minutes of fun, and she got PREGNANT! When the boyfriend finds out she's pregnant, he abandons her and gets another girlfriend. When his eighteenth birthday arrives – he gets a birthday present he'll never forget – a paternity lawsuit. Bill explains to the audience the various ways the boy's paternity can be established. Now, the boy needs a job to pay child support every month. And guess where ninety-five percent of all audiences want the boy to work? Yep, McDonalds! On the dry-erase board, Bill gives him a starting salary of $1,000 per month. When the income taxes, child support, cell phone bill, gasoline, and other monthly expenses are paid for – he's BROKE! Bill shows the audience how the couple's few minutes of fun has now cost the young man over $100,000 during the next eighteen years of his life. Due to additional laws being passed by the Texas legislature, Bill added those laws to his presentation and changed the name of the program to *'Sex and the Law'* in 1995, to educate teen males on their responsibility and accountability regarding sex.

Bill presented this program at conferences for teachers, school counselors, principals, superintendents, and school board members, and he still does. It is his most requested presentation. When school districts call requesting either the *'Child Safety'* or the *'Sex and the Law'* program, Bill always suggests both programs to educate all students. Most school districts are small and Bill is able to present one *'Sex and the Law'* program to the high school students and one *'Sex and the Law'* program to all of the junior high school students. Then he presents a twenty-minute *'child safety'* program to pre-k and kindergarten students, one thirty-minute *'child safety'* program to all of the first and second-grade students, and a forty-five-minute program to third, fourth, and fifth-grade students. The principals and counselors love Bill's schedule. Larger districts obviously require more time and days.

Some districts wanted permission slips from parents for their child to attend Bill's programs. With parents not knowing the positive content of Bill's program, the permission form was a bad idea. Bill felt the permission slip was another way for Satan to keep students from attending his program. So, Bill devised his own form. It was a 'Non-Permission' form. The form for the elementary students basically said to parents, if they do not want their child to attend Bill's safety program and hear information from 'Officer Bill' that could save their child's life then sign the form at the bottom and return it to the school. The junior high school and high school forms basically say to parents, if they do not want their sons to learn about laws that might keep them out of prison, and if they do not want their daughters to learn about laws that might keep them from getting pregnant, then

LOOK OUT SATAN ~ GOD'S AT WORK!

sign the form at the bottom and return it to the school. Rarely is a 'Non-Permission' form returned.

A friend came to Bill one day with a thought. Bill's *'Sex and the Law'* program was ninety minutes long. His friend mentioned that teenagers seeing his program might retain five percent of his presentation. Bill quickly sat down at his computer and took every law and important detail mentioned in his presentation and put it in a 8 ½" x 11" tri-fold brochure. At the end of each program (or the next day), each student receives a brochure. The brochure also has Bill's contact information. Now, if a student has a question, Bill is only a phone call away. And, Beaumont P.D. never paid for one brochure. Bill paid for every one of them.

One day Bill was working an extra job when a man approached him and inquired about his programs. Bill shared one of his *'Sex and the Law'* brochures with the man and explained his teenager's program in more detail with the documented laws he pointed out in the brochure. The man mentioned that it was great that the city supported Bill and his programs by printing the brochures for him. Bill quickly corrected the man and told him that he paid for the printing of the brochures, not the city. The man then asked Bill if he would like to have a sponsor to help with the costs of his programs. Bill could not believe what he was hearing. God had placed this man in Bill's path to help Bill reach even more teenage lives. Through the years, this sponsor, a group of military veterans, has helped Bill with thousands of dollars for brochures, equipment, and other items needed to get his message to students with the hope of saving a life. All Bill could do was thank the Lord, once again, for making his programs even better.

Bill was driving to a speaking engagement and was thinking of his programs. He was educating professionals, law enforcement personnel, child protective services personnel, and others about child abuse. He was educating elementary students about safety issues. He was educating teenagers about *'Sex and the Law.'* Suddenly, that quiet, small voice said one word, 'parents.' Bill was leaving out an entire group of people when he visits a community – Parents! Bill's habit as he arrives at a school district is to always go directly to the office of the teacher, counselor, or principal who invited him to the district and let them know he arrived safely. He would then go to his hotel and rest from his trip.

After this particular speaking trip, Bill spent the next few weeks designing a slide presentation catering to parents. When finished, the program was two-hours long. As school districts called Bill asking him to speak to their students, he gave them a bonus. Yes, he charged the district a fee for speaking to their students. But, he also told them about the two-hour parent night program. It was free, and his way of saying "Thank You" to the district for allowing him the privilege of speaking to their students. Bill opened the door for parents to have access to him and have an opportunity to ask any questions they may have about the programs he would present to their children the next day. He also opened their eyes to their legal responsibilities to their children, the school district, and to themselves. Most parents have no idea that under a Texas law, they can be sued for up to $50,000 plus court costs, if their child is documented as a bully, and as parents, they were advised of their child's negative behavior, but it was not corrected.

Many law enforcement agencies in the area where Bill has presented his programs have their officers attend the two-hour parent presentation for the legal information Bill provides and receive two hours of in-service training. As Bill finishes his programs in a school district and heads home, he is always physically tired, but emotionally pleased that the Lord has presented him with an opportunity to educate professional first responders, parents, school administrators, school staff, and students. His hope and prayer are always that his words to parents help them be better parents. His hope and prayer is always that his words to elementary students help keep them safe and always help them choose the right decisions when everyone else is making the wrong decisions. His hope and prayer for teenagers is that they always make the right moral and legal decisions when confronting sexual experiences.

A program coordinator from Corpus Christi, Texas, sat through one of Bill's presentations at a state conference. She approached him and asked if he would be willing to be a guest speaker for her as she booked seminars throughout the nation. "Of course," he responded. A few months later she called Bill and asked if he would like to present an abbreviated three-hour version of his eight-hour child abuse seminar to approximately six-hundred child daycare, pre-k, and kindergarten teachers in Newark, New Jersey. He quickly accepted her offer.

The date to fly to Newark finally arrived. The next morning, the programs with Bill and another motivational speaker began. Bill poured his Texas heart out to his group of three-hundred teachers. After his first three-hour presentation, one of the teachers approached him and made a profound statement to Bill. In her Jersey lingo, she said, "Sgt. Davis, you talk so fast I couldn't take notes. Do you have a pamphlet, or booklet, or something like that to help me remember all the things you said?" "No, ma'am. I'm sorry," he replied. Bill was sad that he could not accommodate the lady's request. He presented his second program, and his group flew back to Texas the next morning. On the flight back, the lady's words would not go away. Bill regretted that he did not think about preparing a pamphlet or booklet to provide his audience with documentation for current and future notes about child abuse. God's quiet, small voice had planted another seed.

Bill returned home and immediately went to work on his new project. He reviewed his child abuse awareness program slides and documented the programs. He opened his Texas law book and began quoting Texas laws as they pertain to child abuse and child abuse investigations. Bill included child physical abuse indicators as well as the profiles of abusers. With sexual abuse, he included the profiles of rapists and child molesters. Bill wanted to educate everyone that read his booklet of appropriate laws pertaining to the four kinds of child abuse. He also wanted to educate people on how to recognize predators who walk amongst us. Through this education, Bill hoped more children's lives would be saved. His small pamphlet turned into a 90-page booklet and he gave it the title of his child abuse seminar, *'Child Abuse: A National Epidemic.'* Bill updated his original booklet and it is now a 127-page booklet. (If the pages were turned sideways to the size of a normal book page, the booklet would be a 244-page book or more.) Many school districts have requested Bill to present his in-service child abuse program, as required by a Texas law passed in 2003, to all of their staff members and asked that he supply everyone with his booklet. Many law enforcement agencies and police academies have made the same request. He also has his booklet available to anyone at his booth at trade shows. Thousands of booklets have been sold throughout Texas and the nation as another tool to save children's lives.

Here are a few examples of the results of the programs God gave Bill to present to students:

(1) Bill has had the honor of speaking at school districts in the Texas Panhandle many times. On one of those occasions, he was speaking at an elementary school. As he reached the last part of the program and was talking about 'good touches and bad touches' and what 'Officer Bill' calls the 'Uh-Oh touch,' he told the children if someone ever does the 'uh-oh' touch to them that they should go and tell someone they trust. A few seconds later as Bill continued with his program, he noticed a girl about seven years old get out of her seat and walk to her teacher. He noticed them whispering to each other. The teacher then got out of her seat and walked out of the auditorium holding the girl's hand. Bill finished his program a few minutes later. He walked into the principal's office and learned the girl made an outcry about being sexually molested by some older boys at the elementary school in the girl's restroom and the same boys sexually molested her at a friend's birthday party at the friend's

house a few days earlier. Bill personally notified the police chief of that town because the principal refused to make the report, citing that she didn't want to cause problems in her school and community. The chief conducted a criminal investigation on the boys because they were all ten years old or older. As Bill was driving home, he realized that this little girl only made her outcry because Officer Bill told her she had his permission to go and tell someone she trusted and his permission was greater than anyone else's permission. As he drove, he thanked the Lord for placing him and his program at that school for the little girl and others to hear.

(2) Bill was invited to a school district north of Houston by the law enforcement agency that provided police officers for security at the school district. Bill spoke to the parents the night before the student presentations. The next day, he presented programs to the district's students from pre-k through high school seniors. As Bill finished the last program, he loaded up his equipment in his vehicle and drove home. Four days later, Bill's phone rang. The girl calling Bill told him he was at her school district a few days earlier and she heard his program with the junior high school students. She told him she did not know who to trust but felt she could trust him. She began telling him about her stepfather and how he beat up her mom "all the time." The girl said she and her older brother always tried to protect their mom but he beat them up, too. As she continued talking about this abusive man, Bill could hear her voice trembling. Finally, Bill said to her, "Tell me what he has been doing to you." The phone went silent. A few seconds later, Bill could hear the girl quietly crying. Slowly she began telling Bill the stepfather would come into her room during the night and sexually molest her. Bill frantically began taking notes. They talked for several more minutes. He assured the girl she had done the right thing in calling him and she had done nothing wrong. As the call ended, Bill immediately called the officer that invited him to the school district and told him about the girl's outcry. The officer was familiar with the stepfather. He was a suspected drug

dealer in their community. The officer got busy on the investigation. He called Bill a week later. The domestic violence and sexual abuse allegations were basically a 'he said – she said' situation. However, their department was able to arrest the stepfather for distribution of a controlled substance through an undercover officer, and due to the stepfather's extensive criminal record, he would be in jail and prison for a long time. Bill had the opportunity to present his programs at the young girl's school district. She trusted Bill enough to seek his help. In the end, her sexual abuse stopped and the domestic violence in her home stopped because God used Bill and his programs to help this girl, and possibly others.

(3) Christmas was rapidly approaching one year. Bill was invited to speak at a private school two days before the Christmas break. The private school only taught grades pre-k through eighth grade. He began the day by presenting his three versions of *'Child Safety: First & Forever with Officer Bill'* to the pre-k through fifth-grade students. He finished the day with his ninety-minute *'Sex and the Law'* program to the sixth through eighth-grade students. He then packed his equipment in his vehicle and headed home. The school was several hundred miles from Beaumont and Bill stopped along the way and spent the night. He drove throughout the next day, arriving home shortly before 4:00 p.m. As he was unloading his vehicle, his home phone rang. He answered and a young male voice asked to speak to Sgt. Bill Davis. Bill told him he was speaking. The young man told Bill he had spoken at his school the day before. The young man had evidently gotten Bill's telephone number from the *'Sex and the Law'* brochure that all students received after the presentation. Bill was used to getting phone calls from teenagers after presenting a program at their school and asking him questions. So, Bill thanked the young man for calling and then asked him what his question was. The young man promptly told Bill he didn't have a question. He said he wanted to tell Bill something. Bill told him to go ahead and quietly listened. The young man told Bill that he and his girlfriend were in the

eighth grade. They had both professed to be in love with one another. The boy continued by telling Bill that he and his girlfriend were so much in love that they decided to give themselves to each other (have sexual intercourse) that night after school as a Christmas present to each other. The young man then said to Bill, "And then you had to go and do that stupid program yesterday." He continued telling Bill that after school, instead of going to their secret place and having sex, they both agreed that what they heard in the presentation made sense. He told Bill that he and his girlfriend agreed that if they really loved each other, they could wait until they got married one day and then they could have lots of sex. Bill could hardly contain himself. He told the young man, "You didn't make my day. You made my year!" They talked for a few more minutes and the conversation ended. Bill sat in his chair at his desk and looked up at the ceiling. All he could think of was to thank God for giving him the opportunity to present a program for that young man and his girlfriend and others to hear. He never knew if the young man and his girlfriend maintained their virginity and practiced abstinence until they were married, but there was one thing he did know. He knew the program God gave him to share with teenagers stopped these two junior high school teenagers from going through with their sexual plans the night before. 'Wow! What a Christmas gift!' Bill thought, as he smiled and leaned back in his chair.

 (4) Another speaking engagement took Bill to a school district west of Fort Worth. He presented his parent night program the evening he arrived at the school district. The next day he began his programs for all of the students in the district. The high school presentation placed him in front of several hundred teenagers. As he finished the presentation, it was lunchtime for the students. About ten to twelve students stayed in the auditorium with Bill to ask him questions. He was tired and sat on the edge of the stage drinking a bottle of water as he listened and answered their questions, one at a time. As he answered each question, the student or group of students wanting an

answer to the same question, left the auditorium and hurried to the cafeteria for lunch.

The last student was a beautiful young lady. She could have easily adorned the cover of a women's magazine. As her fellow students left, Bill turned his attention to her and asked her what her question was. She suddenly burst into tears. Bill immediately jumped down from the stage and quickly sat beside her. She turned to him and buried her face in his shoulder and wept. He put his arms around her and let her cry. As her tears slowly subsided, she told him it was her fault. "We'll see. Tell me what happened," he asked. As she slowly began talking, Bill realized this precious young lady had not told her story to anyone. He recognized this girl felt that Bill was the only person in the world she could talk to about what happened. He listened intently. She began telling him that she went to a friend's house the weekend prior. Two more teenage girls and two teenage boys showed up at the friend's house. One of the boys brought some drugs and liquor. She said she didn't do drugs, but she didn't want to be an outcast, so she went along with the crowd and drank some of the liquor. She told Bill that a few minutes later, she began to feel very woozy and sleepy. One of the boys volunteered to take her to one of the bedrooms to lie down. As she lay on the bed, he began to undress her and sexually fondle her. She said he was trying to rape her. She continued to tell Bill it was her fault and that she should not have had any alcohol that night. Bill assured her that it was not her fault. He told her she had been targeted by the boy to be a sex crime victim. She told him she was able to fight him off until he got frustrated and left the room. She said she was able to get out of bed and lock the bedroom door before she collapsed in bed and slept the rest of the night. Bill asked her if the drug brought to the party was 'Rohypnol', commonly known as the 'date-rape' drug. She said, "Yes." He explained that this was a drug smuggled into the U.S. from Mexico and was probably slipped into her drink. He then advised her to go to the police station that afternoon after school and report the incident. She said she didn't know if she could do that. She said her fellow students might make fun of her. Bill then asked her a simple question, "Do you think you are the first girl this guy has done this to?" She sat silently. He then asked her another question, "Do you think you are going to be the last girl he tries to rape?" He then asked her one last question "Do you want to put a stop to his perverted acts and protect other girls?" He was doing his best to empower her and help her to go from being a victim to a survivor, to an overcomer. She said he helped her feel better about what happened and she would think about going to the police that afternoon. She left the auditorium. Bill was not far behind her. He was hungry and had more programs to present to other students after lunch.

Bill completed his programs that afternoon, loaded his equipment in his vehicle, and started driving home. He was driving south on Interstate-45 when his cell phone rang. It was almost 5:00 p.m. He answered the phone and a female voice was on the other end of the call. She asked if she was speaking to Sgt. Bill Davis. He replied, "Yes." The young lady told him her name. He recognized the name as the young lady who had been the last person to talk to him after he presented his *'Sex and the Law'* program to the high school students. However, he noticed this girl's voice did not sound sad. She sounded excited. She told him she got the courage to go to the police station to report the boy that attempted to sexually assault her a few days earlier. She said she was prepared for the officers to degrade her. Instead, they were excited to see her. The officers told her they had been hearing about this guy for some time and how he allegedly drugged teenage girls and then tried to rape, or did rape them. Until now, no one had the courage to make an outcry and was willing to give a statement until she walked through the door. She told Bill she gave a detective a sworn statement and the names of everyone else that were at the party. The detective assured her the suspect would be in jail in a matter of hours. Bill was so excited for her. He even remarked, "I don't think this is the same girl that was crying on my shoulder a few hours ago." She quickly exclaimed, "No sir, it's not!"

As they ended their conversation, Bill could not stop smiling. The school's counselor invited Bill to present his program for teenagers after she saw him present it at a Texas counselors' conference. He had the honor of presenting his program to an auditorium packed with hundreds of teenagers and he hoped his program made a positive difference to many of the students. He answered questions for several students. He emboldened one teenage girl to not succumb to being a victim. He encouraged her to help stop a rapist. She did.

(5) A high school teacher who saw Bill present his *'Sex and the Law'* program at her state conference convinced her principal and superintendent that their students needed to hear Bill's programs. Their district only had about 800 students. Their community was an old Texas town that dated back to the Texas Revolution period. The community had a hotel that was often frequented by General/President/Governor Sam Houston back in the 1800s. Bill began the day with his ninety-minute program for the district's high school students. The setting for the program was the district's gym. As he finished the high school program they exited through doors on one side of the gym and the junior high school students entered through the opposite doors of the gym. Bill began their program as soon as they were all seated. He knew he was on a tight schedule because he was to eat lunch in the junior high/high school counselor's office after the program and then present his three programs for the elementary students as soon as he finished his lunch. He began their program with his powerpoint slides and got their attention. He told them he was there to talk to them about an interesting topic – SEX! Suddenly, all the students were laughing and wondering what this man in a police uniform was going to say next. Bill continued and a couple of minutes later, he showed a slide that stated, "One in three females will be sexually misused in some manner before they enter high school." He followed that slide with another one that stated, "One in six males will be sexually misused in some manner before they enter high school." Bill told

the students that the sexual perpetrator is usually not a stranger. He told them that most of the time the perpetrator is someone they know, usually someone they trust, and usually live with. He told them if he was talking to someone described in these slides, to go and talk to someone they trust and tell them what happened to them. Suddenly, a young lady stood up in the middle of the gym seats, stepped down through several students, and walked out of the gym. Bill never broke stride with his program, although he wondered if she suddenly needed to go to the bathroom. He finished the program about an hour later. A few minutes later he entered the counselor's office, ready for lunch. Sitting in a chair by the counselor's desk was the young lady who had gotten up and exited the gym. The counselor was sitting behind her desk. She looked up at Bill as he entered and said to him, "We need your help. You told our students to go and tell someone if they are a victim of what you were talking about. This girl, Amy (pseudonym name), came into my office and began crying and telling me about her father having sex with her. Bill, what do we do?" Bill calmly walked over to Amy and sat in a chair beside her. He touched her forearm and began telling her how proud he was of her telling someone what was happening to her. He looked at the counselor and suggested that she call the sheriff's department. He further suggested that a female deputy be sent. The counselor immediately made the call. Bill assured Amy that she had done nothing wrong and everything was going to be all right. The counselor then escorted Bill to another room of her office so he could eat his lunch. He finished lunch a few minutes later. As he walked into the main room of the counselor's office, two female deputies were entering the room. Bill introduced himself to the deputies and told them about Amy's outcry. They told him they would take over from that point and they would take good care of Amy. One of the deputies gave Bill her email address. He would need to do some paperwork for Amy's investigation because he and his program instigated Amy's outcry. Three elementary student programs later and Bill was driving home. All he could think of as he was driving was to thank the Lord for the opportunity to save one more life.

(6) A counselor at a school district north of Lufkin called Bill and scheduled him to present his programs to the students of her district. On the day of the programs, Bill's schedule was the opposite of how he usually presented his programs. He usually began the day with his program to high school students and then the schedule was fluid from there. This day, he began with the program for junior high school students. He presented two elementary student programs before lunch and one after lunch. The day's schedule ended with Bill's *'Sex and the Law'* program in the high school gym for the high school students. The district's high school was larger than most high schools and the gym was packed. As Bill began the presentation, he noticed a group by the main exit door. They appeared to be parents who came to hear his program. He presented the program with all of the passion and emotion he could muster, as he usually did. As he finished, the high school principal took the microphone from Bill and told all of the students to stay seated. Bill exited the gym floor and walked to where the parents were standing. The principal then added his comments to Bill's program by telling the students he hoped they took what Bill told them to heart. He told them the information in Bill's program could save them a lifetime of problems if they followed his advice. As the principal was ending his comments, a man who appeared to be in his late thirties or early forties walked up beside where Bill was standing. He told Bill he was the father of one of the students and he came to hear what Bill had to say to his child. He ended his conversation with Bill by saying, "It should be mandatory for every high school student in Texas to hear your program as a requirement to graduate high school!" Bill shook the man's hand and thanked him for the compliment. 'Wow!' Bill thought, 'God's at work!'

CHILD ABUSE:
A NATIONAL EPIDEMIC

**The cover of Bill's 127-page booklet,
<u>Child Abuse:</u> <u>A National Epidemic</u>**

**By
Sgt. Bill Davis**

Vol. 2, No. 49 — NEIGHBORHOOD NEWS & VIEWS — 50 Cents

BEAUMONT Journal

Unlocking the 'hidden secret'

April is Child Abuse Awareness Month — page 4

This week
March 26 - April 1, 1998

First-hand viewpoint: Journal writer tries new beauty treatment/**Page 6**

Entertainment: Beaumont Passion Play begins three-day run/**Page 8**

History Journal: Heritage Society opens David French House/**Page 10**

People at Play: Central HS long jump champ joins relay team/**Page 16**

INDEX
Arts & Entertainment	Page 8-9
Classified	Page 21-23
Contemplation Station	Page 20
Editorial	Page 10
History Journal	Page 10
Other Views	Page 12-13
Out and About	Page 7
People at Play	Page 16-18
Photo Gallery	Page 19
School Days	Page 14-15

Weekly *Chuckle*
Some people wait until April 1 to play the fool, but most of us spread it throughout the entire year.

District Judge Jimmy "Skip" Hulett Jr., Sexual Assault Nurse Examiner, Brenda Garison, Sgt. Bill Davis, Dr. Maxie Sprott II

All adorn the front page of the Beaumont Journal March 26, 1998. Unlocking the 'hidden secret' is the feature story of this issue of the Journal.

Vol. 1, No. 33 — NEIGHBORHOOD NEWS & VIEWS — 50 Cents

BEAUMONT Journal

This week
December 5-11, 1996

Success Story: Local gunsmith turns hobby into full-time job/**Page 4**

In the News: Luncheon raises more than $100,000 for breast cancer project/**Page 10**

Neighbors: Habitat for Humanity starts nine new homes/**Page 18**

People at Play: Two local gymnasts advance to state finals/**Page 20**

INDEX
Arts and Entertainment	9
Achievements	5
Classified	Page 24-27
Contemplation Station	Page 23
Editorial	Page 14
History Journal	Page 14
Neighbors	Page 8, 10, 18
Other Views	16-17
Out and About	Page 13
People at Play	Page 19-21
Photo Gallery	Page 22
School Days	11

Weekly *Chuckle*
Appearances can be deceiving. After all, the dollar looks just the same as it did 10 years ago.

'If we can save one child...'

Policeman fights sex crimes with education — pg. 6

THE GARTH HOUSE
MICKEY MEHAFFY CHILDREN'S ADVOCACY PROGRAM

Bill is on the front page of the Beaumont Journal December 5, 1996, and the feature story was Bill's effort to increase awareness about sex crimes through education.

Chapter Twelve

God Really Does Work In Mysterious Ways!

God really has worked, and is still working in exciting and mysterious ways through Bill's life. Some of these mysterious ways seemed normal at first, but were extraordinary and helped and protected Bill. Other exciting incidents have placed him in someone's path to help them through what seemed to be impossible circumstances.

Bill had the honor of presenting his *'Child Safety: First & Forever with Officer Bill'* program to students at a private school in Beaumont during the fall semester of 1990. These programs were especially exciting for Bill because Dusty was a student at this school. Bill was at the mall one evening several days later. He was standing in the southern walkway of the mall smoking a cigarette while his family was in one of the stores shopping. Suddenly he heard a child's voice calling his name, "Officer Bill, Officer Bill!" He turned in the child's direction. He did not recognize the child, but he did recognize the school shirt the child was wearing as one of the uniform shirts from Dusty's school. The little boy ran ahead of his parents to greet his police officer friend. Bill's hand was level with the boy's head and he immediately saw the cigarette between Bill's fingers. The little boy gasped in shock and said, "Officer Bill, you smoke!" Bill was very embarrassed. He had just made a very negative impact on a little boy. He quickly disposed of the cigarette and knelt in front of this child. He told the little boy that smoking was very bad and hoped he never smoked. He also thanked the little boy for being a great listener at his program several days earlier. The little boy's parents caught up with the pair, thanked Bill for his work with children, got their son, and walked on. The little boy's words would not go away.

Bill knew that smoking was bad for his health, but he did it anyway. He was forty years old and had smoked cigarettes since he was eighteen. But that evening, he, Officer Bill, made a negative impact on a young boy. He worried during the next days and weeks, hoping the little boy never smoked cigarettes. He worried that his smoking would someday have a negative impact on his own son and he would start smoking because of his dad's bad influence. Bill tried to quit smoking on his own but couldn't seem to do it. Finally, someone mentioned to Bill that hypnosis might be the assistance he needed to kick the habit. He found a hypnotist in Beaumont's north end and made an appointment. As he approached the building for his hypnotic session, a trash can was outside the front door. Bill reached in his pocket, pulled out his pack of cigarettes, threw it in the trash, and walked into the hypnotist's office. As the session ended an hour later, Bill wondered if he had really been hypnotized. The hypnotist had recorded the session, gave Bill a cassette tape of it, and told him to listen to the recording every night when he went to bed. He was to do this for several weeks. It was January 1991. He did as the hypnotist told him, falling asleep every night for several weeks, listening to the recording. He found out later that falling asleep while listening to the tape was called 'self-hypnosis.' Bill never smoked again. God had used the voice of a little boy to save Bill from possible death due to lung cancer, heart attack, stroke, or other disease related to smoking. To this day, over thirty-one years later, Bill is thankful he listened to that little boy.

Bill retired from the Beaumont Police Department on January 31, 2008. He wanted to remain a Texas law enforcement officer as he had been for almost thirty-six years. A friend who was also a sheriff in a nearby county began carrying Bill's Texas law enforcement commission the day after Bill's retirement. A couple of different agencies have carried his state law enforcement commission through his years of retirement. To date, he is still a law enforcement officer for the State of Texas. Bill proudly wears his Texas peace officer uniform when presenting school programs and at other functions that afford him the opportunity to show the world that he is still a police officer.

Bill was at the workbench in his garage one day working on a project. The garage door was open and he suddenly heard a man cursing at the top of his voice. He walked onto his driveway and could tell the cursing was coming from someone at the house across the street. Bill could also see clothes being thrown from the front door of the house onto the lawn. Bill got his pepper spray from the door panel of his truck and walked into the street to better observe what was going on. As he walked toward the home's front yard but stayed in the middle of the street, he saw a bearded man standing on his front porch, cursing at the top of his lungs at a petite young woman who was frantically picking up the clothes from off the grass. Bill also observed children riding bicycles along the intersecting street, hearing the man's vulgarity. As Bill stood in the street, the man looked his way. "Hey, that's enough," Bill said in a calm but commanding voice to the bearded man. He began cursing at Bill, telling Bill to get lost. Bill quietly told the man it was a public street and he would stand there all day if he wanted to. The man started walking toward Bill in an angry manner. This diversion gave the young woman time to finish gathering her clothes, get her children into their vehicle, and leave this horrible situation. The man jumped the ditch between his yard and the street where Bill was standing. The man was suddenly within a foot of Bill's face cursing and screaming. Bill never moved. He quietly told the man he was a police officer and the Groves Police Department was on the way. The man angrily told Bill he was going to stomp his butt (not the word he used). Bill's reply was simply, "Don't touch me. You'll regret it." The man was so close to Bill that he did not see Bill slowly remove the pepper spray from his pocket, ready to defend himself. When Bill didn't move, the man jumped back across the ditch, still cursing Bill, and walked into his house.

A few minutes later, four Groves P.D. officers arrived at the man's house. A short time later, one of the officers came to Bill's home. As he and Bill began talking, they both reminisced, knowing each other from many years earlier and growing up in the same church in the Groves area. The officer then told Bill that the man causing the problem was a Marine veteran named, Stephen, who had served in the Afghanistan war and suffered from Post Traumatic Stress Disorder. The officer said they had been called to the man's house on at least three or four occasions on similar incidents. Bill told the officer he wanted to file disorderly conduct charges on Stephen. Bill completed the necessary paperwork and the officer left.

The next morning, that quiet, small voice began speaking to Bill. He began wondering how he could help Stephen instead of filing charges against him. Bill was asked a few years earlier by a nephew if he would like to work the Frog Festival in Crystal Beach, Texas. The nephew, Brandon, was a Marine and Seal team veteran and was co-owner of a security company. Bill was honored to be part of a crew of former military men. The proceeds of this festival were to help the Lone Survivor Foundation build a therapy complex in Crystal Beach on property donated by a local building contractor. The complex was to help veterans suffering from PTSD and their families. Bill worked the festival for three years and had the honor of meeting Marcus Luttrell, the lone survivor, on two of those occasions. Bill also had the honor of providing security for Marcus and the contractor as they held the ground-breaking ceremony for the therapy complex. The following year as Bill worked the festival, the contractor gave him a tour of the new facility. He showed Bill one of the main therapy locations, the fire pit in the middle of the complex. The contractor explained how many veterans attending the facility for help solved many PTSD problems sitting and talking with other veterans around the fire pit throughout the night.

As the good Lord put these thoughts in Bill's head, he made a couple of phone calls and got a phone number for the therapy complex. He then spent the rest of his morning working on some 'honey-do's' outside his house. While working, he suddenly heard, "Mr. Bill, can I talk to you?" Bill looked and saw the person calling him was Stephen standing in the street by his driveway. Bill invited him forward saying, "Come on up." As they met, Stephen extended his hand of friendship and apologized to Bill for his conduct the day before. Bill told Stephen he filed criminal charges against him for his conduct. Stephen stated he deserved those charges and he would gladly pay the fine. Bill reached in his pocket and pulled out a sheet of paper with a phone number on it. He explained to Stephen that the Groves P.D. Officer told him about Stephen's battle with PTSD. Bill told Stephen how God spoke to him that morning. He told Stephen about the Lone Survivor Foundation facility only a short distance away in Crystal Beach. Bill then made Stephen a promise. He told Stephen that if he would begin the process of getting therapy for his PTSD through the Lone Survivor Foundation, he would drop the charges against him. They shook hands on it. The deal was made.

Stephen and Bill met several times and began a great friendship. Stephen informed Bill one day that he received a notice of his court date from the Groves Municipal Court. Bill made a note of the date. On that day, Bill picked Stephen up from his house and drove him to the municipal court. On the way, Stephen gave Bill an update on when he was to go to the Lone Survivor Foundation facility for therapy. When they arrived at the court office, Bill dropped the charges against his new friend.

Bill and Stephen visited every time they were both outside their homes at the same time. Several months after their first encounter, Stephen excitedly told Bill how wonderfully his therapy at the complex was and how it was making a positive difference in his life. He also told Bill his name was already added to the waiting list for a 'couples' therapy session through the foundation for him and his wife. Several weeks later, Stephen and Amber told Bill the couples retreat was transformative for them as individuals and as a couple.

As Christmas 2021 approached, Bill and his wife of three years, Cheryl, made out Christmas cards for many friends and relatives. Stephen and his family no longer lived across the street from Bill and Cheryl. They moved a few blocks away. Bill drove to their new residence and presented Stephen with a Christmas card for their family. When Bill asked how they were doing, Stephen excitedly told Bill about their couple's therapy trip and how positively it helped Amber and him. He continued by telling Bill how his brother from Michigan and his wife also went to the Lone Survivor Foundation's therapy complex for their couple's therapy session. He told several of his fellow military brothers about the foundation and they had also gone for PTSD help from the Lone Survivor Foundation because of his recommendation. As Bill left Stephen's home, all he could do was thank God for helping our veterans. And it all started with a nephew asking Bill to be a part of his security team at the Frog Festival years earlier. God's work continued through the man cursing and screaming in his front yard. Bill smiled as he drove away. It never ceases to amaze Bill how God can take something horrible, and through others, turn a terrible situation into something for His good. And many times, with a 'ripple' effect to it all.

As of this writing, Amber has applied for attendance at a spouse's retreat through the Lone Survivor Foundation that will be held later this year (2022). The spouse of one of Stephen's Army brothers also applied to attend the spouse's retreat. And, the ripple effect continues.

One of Bill's nieces, Ellie Mae, called him one evening. He could hear the fear in her voice. She said she needed to talk to him, but didn't want him mad at her. He quickly told her he would not be mad at her and she could tell him anything. She began crying. Bill listened. She finally gained enough composure to tell him about a series of negative events that happened to her and she did not know who to call for help, except him. Bill did not know Ellie Mae very well. He was related to her through distant relatives. One day she saw his first book on display in a book stand at a convenience store in Hardin County, Texas. Her aunt bought it for her, telling her as the purchase was made, that Bill Davis was her uncle. After reading the book, she called him asking to come to his home so he could autograph her book. That autograph session was their first meeting. Now, she was desperately seeking his help. She just turned seventeen years old the month before. As she told him of this recent situation, Bill realized that Ellie Mae not only needed his legal advice, but she also needed Cheryl's friendship and their moral support. As the days and weeks went by, Ellie Mae called Bill and Cheryl almost every night. Many of Ellie Mae's phone calls were to just have someone to talk to. As the days and nights went by, Bill and Cheryl learned more and more about Ellie Mae's emotionally and physically abusive childhood. She was desperate for someone to give her positive attention, affection, and love. Ellie Mae's personality slowly began to change to a wonderful outgoing young lady. She now calls Cheryl her 'best friend.'

As time went on, Bill and Cheryl helped Ellie Mae in various ways. She took driver's education in high school. But, when it came time to get her driver's license, no one in her family would take the time or spend the money for Ellie Mae to get her license. Several months went by and Ellie Mae finally had her eighteenth birthday. At this age, she did not need her mother or father to accompany her for her license. Bill and Cheryl agreed to help her. Bill and Cheryl drove forty-five miles from their home early one morning to Ellie Mae's home and picked up the excited teenager. They arrived at the closed driver's license office door at 7:00 a.m. The office didn't open until 8:00 a.m. It was December and it was cold that day. They were hoping to be the first ones in line that morning by arriving so early, but they wound up being second in line. Most of that hour was spent with Cheryl and Ellie Mae sitting in a warm car while Bill held their place in line. Not long after the office doors opened, Bill and Cheryl paid for Ellie Mae's license and the happy teenager left with her driver's license in hand. Her smile wouldn't go away.

Ellie Mae finally finished her senior year. Each graduating senior was allowed to have someone, usually a parent, escort them across the stage to receive their diploma. She asked Bill if he would escort her

LOOK OUT SATAN ~ GOD'S AT WORK!

across the stage in his police uniform. He was honored and proudly escorted her. She was now eighteen years old. She was an adult under criminal and civil law and could live anywhere she wanted. An incident happened at the relative's residence where she was living and her need to move to a safer environment was imperative. Bill discussed Ellie Mae's plight with his best friend, Rick. "I've got an old RV camper that we can renovate and she can use it as her new, safe home while she goes to college," Rick proclaimed. Ellie Mae was all for the idea. A few days later, Bill and Rick were at Rick's camp on his deer lease, confiscating the old camper. The next day, their work began. The camper was in worse shape than Rick thought. The three-week project that Rick guesstimated would restore the camper, turned into an ordeal that lasted several months. Ellie Mae waited patiently while secretly living with a lady and babysitting her children. Realizing that Ellie Mae had a driver's license but no means of transportation prompted Rick and his wife, Cindy, to make a big decision. Rick had an old truck from the '80s. It had no heat or air conditioning, but it ran great. With Bill and Cheryl paying for the title transfer to Ellie Mae's name, Rick handed the keys over to a very grateful young lady. She now had transportation.

    The two men worked tirelessly day after day on the camper, trying to build a home for Ellie Mae. As hurricane season began, Southeast Texas and Southwest Louisiana braced for storms. Two storms hit Southeast Texas within three weeks. As the first storm hit, it damaged six sheets of paneling inside the camper. The two men pooled their money, as they had done throughout the entire project, and bought more paneling. A couple of days later, the new paneling was up and they continued with their renovations. Less than two weeks later, the second storm hit the area. It was worse than the first one. Bill called his friend and inquired about the camper. "You've got to come and see," Rick told Bill. He was at Rick's house within minutes. As he entered the camper, tears filled his eyes. They had caulked every seam in the RV twice. Yet, water or moisture found its way into the camper and mold was on every piece of paneling. It was like God was telling them, "I tried to stop you with the first storm, but y'all wouldn't listen. I have other plans for Ellie Mae."

Bill and Cheryl invited Ellie Mae to go to church with them one Sunday. They knew she had been raised in a different faith than theirs, but realized the worst she could say to them was "no." But, she said "yes." Through Bill and Cheryl taking Ellie Mae to church, she felt Jesus tugging at her heart one Sunday. When the invitation was given, Ellie Mae grabbed the hands of Bill and Cheryl and had them escort her to the front of the church. She made a profession of faith and was baptized two weeks later. Their many Sunday trips of driving almost one-hundred miles to get Ellie Mae, take her to church, take her to lunch, and then take her back home, had paid off. Ellie Mae was now their 'Sister in Christ' forever.

Now that Ellie Mae had the truck from Rick, it saved Bill and Cheryl lots of miles, and she met them at their church on Sundays. But as old vehicles have parts that break, her truck fit the mold. After church and lunch one Sunday, Ellie Mae followed Bill and Cheryl to their home. Bill was definitely not a mechanic, but Ellie Mae only needed him to change a tail light bulb that had gone out. It took Bill a while, but he changed both taillight bulbs for her. When the job was over, they went into the house. Before she said her goodbye to Bill and Cheryl, Ellie Mae turned to her uncle and said, "Uncle Bill, can I hit you?" Bill had lifted weights since he was sixteen years old. He and Cheryl have a mini-gym in the back room of their home. Bill allowed Ellie Mae to hit him in the belly-button area before. His abdominal muscles were hard and he would always tense them before he let her hit him. She thought it was 'cool' to have an uncle as old as Uncle Bill and him be in shape. As Bill prepared himself for the blow, Cheryl said something that drew his attention from being hit. Ellie Mae was ready, and she swung her right fist at Bill's abdomen. Her aim, however, was off. Instead of hitting Uncle Bill around the belly-button, she hit him just below his sternum in the diaphragm.

It hurt. He told her not to hit that high in the abdomen again. She felt bad and apologized to him. She left a few minutes later. It was Sunday, March 7, 2021.

Bill had been hit before in the diaphragm, as most boys and men have. He knew the feeling of the bruised diaphragm should go away in a few days, but it didn't. His abdominal area seemed to be bloated and more sensitive than normal. The pain seemed to increase. On Tuesday, March 16th, Bill began having a stabbing pain below his left ribcage. The pain increased and was now going into his left chest area making it difficult to breathe. He barely slept through the night. Cheryl took him to a medical facility the next morning. Tests were run and at the end of the day, Bill was transferred by ambulance to a hospital in Beaumont instead of being discharged to go home. Over the next seven days, numerous tests and lab work was conducted. On Monday, March 22nd, Bill underwent an exploratory surgery. Bill did begin to wonder what was wrong with him when an oncologist visited him in his hospital room. Still, no one would tell Bill what was wrong. Finally, Bill demanded to be discharged. He told the nurses he was hungry and ready for a decent meal. He was discharged on Tuesday, March 23rd, at 1:00 p.m.

After a good lunch and taking care of a couple of errands, Bill and Cheryl began driving home. Bill enjoyed being chauffeured by his sweet wife, but he suddenly began having a pain just under his right ribcage, similar to the one he had on the left side a week earlier. It kept getting worse. He again experienced a fitful night due to the pain. The next morning the pain had increased into Bill's chest and he was having severe difficulty breathing. This time, Cheryl called an ambulance. He was taken back to the same hospital he was discharged from the day before. As the paramedics were checking Bill into the emergency department of the hospital, Bill looked down the hallway and recognized a nurse practitioner who visited his hospital room several times during the prior week and worked for the surgeon who conducted the exploratory surgery. Bill waved at the nurse and he came running to Bill's gurney. After Bill told him what was wrong, the nurse excused himself and walked away. He returned to Bill's side a couple of minutes later with two sheets of paper in his hand. "Here's what's wrong with you," he said, as he showed Bill the sheets of paper. The report showed the result of the biopsy from specimens of Bill's abdominal lymph nodes that were taken during the exploratory surgery. Cancer! Bill had B-cell lymphoma cancer. Several hours later, Bill was discharged and he and Cheryl went home. They had an answer to what was causing Bill to hurt so terribly. However, the answer opened the door to many more questions.

A receptionist from the office of the oncologist called Bill and set up an appointment. Bill made the appointment, yet wondered if he should go to M.D. Anderson Hospital in Houston. After all, it is one of the top cancer hospitals in the world and only eighty-five miles away. He kept his appointment with the local oncologist. Bill learned that his cancer was one of the easiest cancers to cure. His doctor advised that after six treatments of chemotherapy, one treatment every three weeks, he should be cancer free. "That's all?" Bill asked. The doctor explained that medical science did not know what caused his type of cancer. He further explained to Bill and Cheryl that Bill's type of cancer is usually not discovered until it is in Stage Four, life-threatening, and very difficult to cure. Bill asked the doctor a simple question, "What stage is my cancer in, and how long have I had it?" "You're in 'Stage Two' and you've had it for about two years. That's why your cancer will be easy to cure," the doctor explained.

As Bill lay in bed that night, he recalled thinking over the last two years that he needed to go on a diet or work out more. He thought he was getting fat in his abdomen, but it wasn't that at all. It was cancer. Ellie Mae was not calling Bill and Cheryl as often as she had been. During one phone call, she began crying and said she felt it was her fault that Uncle Bill was in the hospital. As Bill and Cheryl lay in bed that night, that quiet, small voice began to speak to them. They discussed the situation and both realized that Bill's cancer should have gone undetected until it was too late. And yet, it was discovered in its early stages while it was easy to cure. It was discovered early because of one little incident – a punch by Ellie Mae a little too high in Bill's abdomen. The blow angered the cancer cells in his lymph nodes and they exposed themselves. Bill and Cheryl quickly telephoned Ellie Mae, but she didn't answer. Bill couldn't wait. He began texting her, telling her how God used her to save his life. At the end of the text, he thanked her for hitting him.

Bill's chemotherapy was to begin the third Monday in April. But there was a conflict. His son, Dusty, and his sweetheart, Haylee, planned their wedding for Saturday, April 30th. Bill had no idea what effect chemotherapy would have on his body. He was not about to miss his only child's wedding. Their wedding was a beautiful affair. Now that their wedding was over, therapy could begin. It did, Monday, May 3, 2021.

As Bill began chemotherapy, with Cheryl or his friend, Rick, by his side, he made a very big decision. The night before his first chemotherapy session, Bill began to pray. He told the Lord he didn't know what to do about this cancer. He told the Lord the only thing he could think of was to give the problem to Him. After all, the Lord had said, "Cast all your burdens upon Me and I will give you rest." Bill was amazed at the peace and the positive attitude he had from that night going forward. Many times Bill prayed as his therapy continued, telling the Lord he had a tough day. He continued his prayer telling the Lord that he felt Satan was trying to drag him down. Bill told the Lord he gave this cancer problem to Him and he was not taking it back. Bill prayed this prayer many times over the next several months.

The chemotherapy sessions were fairly easy and he realized that these easy sessions were a blessing from God, because chemotherapy is not easy for everyone. All Bill had to do was recline in a chair and fall asleep following an injection of Benadryl and before the chemotherapy medications were administered. However, the three weeks between sessions was a roller coaster ride, both physically and emotionally. The first week after therapy was usually not bad because he was prescribed a heavy dose of prednisone to take for five days, including the day of therapy. In fact, Bill felt like the 'Energizer Bunny' that week. But, the second week was horrible. With the prednisone out of his system, Bill's energy level seemed to 'bottom out.' He had no energy and felt he could barely put one foot in front of the other. His third week seemed to 'level out' and he felt somewhat normal. Then, it was time for another chemotherapy session and for the cycle to start over. After the fifth chemo session, Bill noticed that he felt like he was getting back to his old self (minus his full head of hair). His last chemotherapy session was scheduled for August 23, 2021. He went through some testing the week before and he and Cheryl had a visit with his oncologist that morning prior to the chemotherapy. As the doctor walked into the exam room, Bill could tell he was smiling even though the doctor was wearing his mask (due to the COVID-19 pandemic). He told Bill and Cheryl he had some exciting news for them. Bill responded by saying, "I'm cancer free, aren't I, doctor?" The doctor responded, "Yes you are!" Bill asked, "Does that mean I get to ring the bell?" "Yes, it does," the doctor happily announced.

    Bill went through his last chemotherapy session. As he and Cheryl entered the lobby to exit the building, they saw the bell mounted on a support column in the room. They walked over to the bell and read the "Ringing Out" inscription on a plaque above it. "Ring this bell three times well its toll to clearly say, my treatment's done, this course is run and I am on my way!" (written by Irve Le Moyne). Bill gave his cell phone to Cheryl to video the event. As Bill finished reading the inscription, he took the bell's rope in his hand. Suddenly the bell was ringing one time, two times, three times! The lobby was quiet when Bill and Cheryl entered it. They were oblivious to the fifteen to twenty people who were sitting, waiting for their appointment. As Bill began ringing the bell, everyone in the room began to clap and cheer. After the third ring, Bill turned to the crowd and threw his fists in the air in victory. As he and Cheryl left the building, they commented that everyone who had cheered for him was hoping their day to ring the bell would come soon.

Bill has often wondered why Satan tried to kill him with cancer. In amazement, Bill thought about how Satan tried to kill him once again but God put an innocent young lady in his life and used her to save his life. Bill reminisced about how it all started with this young lady and her aunt purchasing his first true crime book and her being told the author was her uncle. Satan knew Bill had been working on a third manuscript for another book for over twenty years and now he was serious about finishing it. Satan knew that this new book was all about God and how He enjoys using people for His Honor and Glory. God used Bill's encounter with cancer to slow him down and give him time to finish the book's manuscript. So, it looks like all that's left to be said is,

"LOOK OUT SATAN ~ GOD'S AT WORK!"

The 'Energizer Bunny' and 'Superman' helped Bill through his cancer ordeal.

August 23, 2021, Bill had the honor of ringing the bell! He was cancer-free!

Chemotherapy does cause a person to lose their hair during therapy.

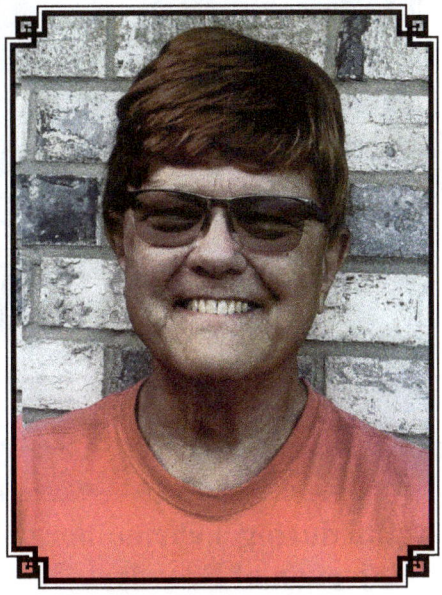

Bill's friend, Carl, provided Bill with a red-haired wig to compensate for his hair loss. "Gee, thanks, Carl!"

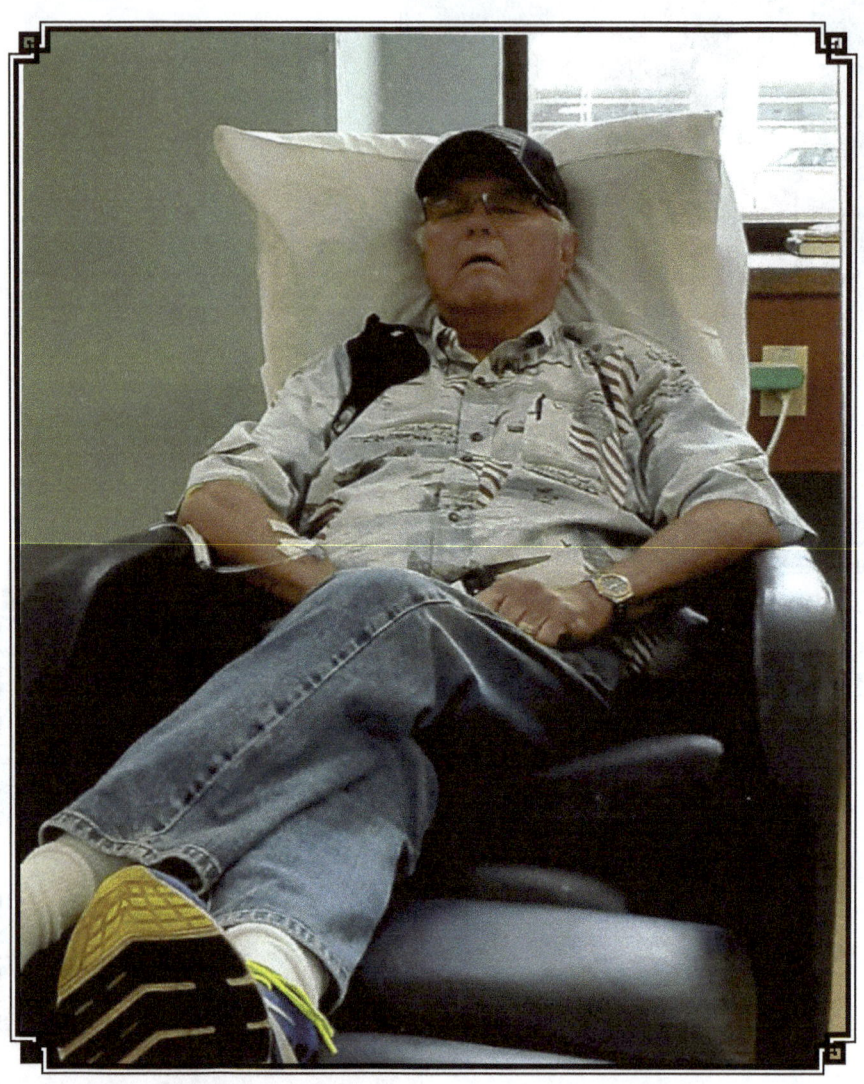

Bill during a chemotherapy session and after an injection of Benadryl.

Epilogue:

So...What <u>Really</u> Happened January 7, 1984?

It was 7:00 a.m. in East Texas that day. Bill and Ron parked the three-wheelers at the old campsite location and began walking down the logging road. They were looking in the trees and on the ground for squirrels. They knew the world was going on around them. However, they were in their own little world enjoying their camaraderie and the start of a day of hunting. What neither of them realized was the argument going on above them – in Heaven. You see, Satan was mad. He was as mad as he could be.

There was this guy named Bill Davis and Satan was griping to Jesus about him. Bill had started investigating child abuse incidents about four years earlier and was putting bad guys in jail for physically hurting and molesting children. Satan let Bill solve those incidents, as he also allowed homicide, robbery, and burglary detectives to solve their crimes so it gave a good appearance everything was going smoothly. Then, Bill began presenting child abuse programs about six months earlier and was saving even more children's lives throughout Southeast Texas. This had to stop. Satan told Jesus he was sick of what Bill was doing and he was putting an end to it. He reminded Jesus it was his job to steal, kill, and destroy. Satan told Jesus this guy, Bill, was getting out of control saving lives, especially with his programs. Satan continued by telling Jesus if he (Satan) didn't stop Bill now, that he would be presenting programs throughout Texas, throughout the United States, and throughout the world!

Satan emphatically told Jesus, "I'm killing him. I'm killing him today!" Jesus looked at Satan with his quiet demeanor and a slight smile on his face. "You think you're in charge, but you're not," Jesus quietly said as He looked Satan in the eyes. Satan couldn't stand the stare and looked down. "You're not killing Bill today. He's one of my boys!" Jesus declared. "See right here," Jesus told Satan, as He held up a big book and pointed to Bill's name. Defiantly, Satan declared again, "Oh, yes I am! I'm killing him just as soon as that squirrel runs up a tree." Jesus chuckled at Satan's stupidity. Satan was not about to acknowledge that Jesus really was in charge – of everything.

"I'm the only one who knows when Bill's time is up on the earth," Jesus told Satan, "and it's not today!" "Oh, yes it is!" Satan screamed at Jesus. With his quiet voice, Jesus looked at Satan and said, "I'll tell you what I will let you do. I will let you hurt him – but you are NOT going to kill him!" "We'll see about that," Satan said defiantly. Jesus ended their conversation by telling Satan, "You're gonna regret this!" as Satan left His presence.

Jesus smiled and called Bill's guardian angel. Jesus assigned a great guardian angel to watch over him. (Bill kept his angel busy guarding him with all of his activities. Bill's bad habit of driving too fast gave him the nickname of 'Bill Davis Airlines' when he was driving a vehicle. Some people even commented to Bill that he needed to slow down so his guardian angel could keep up.) Bill's guardian angel immediately stood in front of Jesus, and Jesus told Bill's angel what was about to happen. He gave specific instructions to Bill's angel that He was going to allow Satan to hurt Bill, but he was not to be killed. Jesus also told Bill's angel that He wanted Bill's injury to be something that would be negative at first, but positive in the long run through the perseverance He had placed in His servant. The angel understood his task – completely!

The squirrel rustling in the leaves to their left and slightly behind them surprised both hunters. They quickly turned around and Ron fired a shot at the squirrel as he crossed the road, now from right to left, about thirty feet from them. He missed. His Remington Model 1100 .12-gauge semi-automatic shotgun quickly loaded another shotgun shell into the chamber. The squirrel ran a few feet into the woods and quickly scampered up a tree. Bill never took his eyes off the tree and started walking toward it from standing beside Ron. As Bill took his third step, an over-hanging limb was in his way and he had to bend down to go under the limb. Common gun safety is simple. Keep the muzzle of your gun pointed up or down, but never at your target until ready to fire.

As Ron was focused on watching Bill, he was unaware that Satan had slowly pointed the muzzle of his powerful shotgun at the middle of Bill's back about six to seven feet away. Satan was smiling. The blast would be lethal. He would have done his job of stealing, killing, and destroying Bill's life. No more programs! No more investigations! No more saving lives by this guy!

Bill's guardian angel was also ready. His angel suddenly made Ron aware of where his gun was pointed. Panic struck Ron. He jerked the barrel of his shotgun from being pointed at the middle of Bill's back to the right as fast as he could. In doing so, Ron pushed the forestock of the gun to the right with his left hand. At the same time, he pulled the shotgun to the right with his right hand, but with his index finger still touching the trigger.

Ron didn't feel his finger pull the trigger. Satan did that for him. Ron only felt the recoil. Bill's angel was ready. Bill had been holding his shotgun with the muzzle pointed downward and his right arm to his side. If Ron's shotgun had fired at that moment, Bill would have been shot in the back and died. But, that wasn't God's plan. If Ron's shotgun had fired a fraction of a second later, Bill would have been shot in the middle of his right arm, losing it and losing his job as a police officer. That wasn't God's plan either.

As Bill lowered the top half of his body to walk under the limb, his right arm moved away from his body with his forearm parallel to the ground. The muzzle of his shotgun was now pointed up and the stock was pointed downward. In what was probably one-ten-thousandth-of-a-second and as the barrel of Ron's gun was moving rapidly to the right and firing, Bill's angel directed seventeen of the #6 shotgun pellets into Bill's right forearm and hand leaving a gaping six-inch gash in his right forearm and losing his right thumb. Four of the pellets ricocheted off the metal of Bill's shotgun hitting him in the abdomen. Bill's guardian angel had successfully done as God instructed him to do. Bill was hurt, but not killed. Satan was furious! He lost! God was at work! God won!

Through several surgeries, nine of the seventeen pellets in Bill's forearm were removed. Eight pellets remain there. Removing them would possibly damage nerves the pellets are close to. Dr. Riordan's reconstruction surgery left a small thumb for Bill. He is still right-hand-oriented. He shoots his guns with his right hand very well, writes right-handed, and is strong with his right hand. However, dealing with small buttons and untying knots can sometimes test his patience.

When 'Officer Bill' is at schools presenting programs or at trade shows selling his books, children think it's 'cool' to touch the nub of his right thumb and also give him a 'High Four.' Three of the four pellets in Bill's abdomen were removed. A fourth pellet surfaced about four inches below his sternum several months later. He could have had it removed with a local anesthetic and a minor incision. But he didn't. That quiet, small voice told him, "Leave it." Bill rubs that pellet almost daily saying, "Thank you, Lord," knowing it was through God's intervention that he is alive today. That pellet is an acknowledgment to Bill that he should have died on January 7, 1984 at 7:05 a.m.

At elementary schools, Bill talks about gun safety and other life-saving topics. At the end of the program, Bill always gives each student an 'Officer Bill's Junior Officer' sticker badge for being great listeners, and they wear the badge proudly. As the students exit the assembly, many of them want to touch Bill's right thumb. One day Bill was wearing regular clothes and was at a mall when he heard a child's voice hollering, "Officer Bill!" He looked around and saw a boy about six years old holding onto his mom's hand and pulling her toward him. "See, mom, I told you his friend shot his thumb off!" the little boy exclaimed. Mom was embarrassed and started apologizing. Bill visited her son's elementary school two days earlier and he came home with his badge and told her all about 'Officer Bill.' Bill told her not to apologize and he knelt in front of the boy. Bill told the smiling young man he was extremely proud of him for listening so well during the program.

At trade shows, Bill is in uniform and he asks children, especially boys, if they would like to feel his bullet. Most do. He unzips his uniform shirt, with a t-shirt underneath, and puts his finger on the bullet (pellet). That bullet then gives him the opportunity to talk to that child about gun safety, not wandering away from their parents, and always wearing their seat belt or sitting in their car seat or booster seat. He then gives that child an *'Officer Bill's Junior Officer'* sticker badge. As 'Officer Bill's' junior officer, he also asks the child to be his helper and make sure that grown-ups and older brothers and sisters buckle up, too. That shotgun pellet, and that nub for a thumb, gives Bill a moment to say a few words that may save a child's life one day.

Thought:
A hundred years from now, it will not matter what your bank account was, the sort of house you lived in, or the kind of car you drove. But, the world may be different because you were important in the life of a child.

A Child's Prayer:
"Dear Lord, be good to me. The sea is so wide and my boat is so small."

Question:
Have you hugged your child today and told him or her, "I Love You?"

Another thought:
I would rather live my life as if there is a God, and die to find out there isn't, than live my life as if there isn't, and die to find out there is!

Last thought:
And through it all...

GOD IS <u>STILL</u>
AT WORK!

A WILLINGNESS TO GET INVOLVED

One evening around 10:00 p.m., a police child abuse detective in one of our Texas communities was at home when his telephone rang. He was needed immediately at one of the local hospitals in reference to a child abuse incident.

Upon arrival at the hospital, he went immediately to the emergency department and was guided to one of the rooms. As he entered, he observed a two-year-old boy lying on the hospital gurney. The seasoned detective reached down and touched the bruised and battered body of the little boy. The child did not move and was cold to the touch. Another one – DEAD!

The care of the child had been entrusted to a boyfriend while the mother worked the evening shift at a local business. The boyfriend, a four-year-old brother to the child, and the child had gone to grandma's house. An aunt was also at the residence. As they entered the home, the boyfriend observed that the two-year-old child had wet his pants. The boyfriend became so infuriated that he began to kick the child with his pointed shoes and beat him with his belt that had a large heavy buckle on the end that was hitting the child. He demanded the older brother clean up the mess. When the brother did not clean up the mess to his satisfaction, he beat the brother, too. After the beatings, he grabbed both boys, exited the home, threw them in the backseat of the car, and drove away. The two-year-old boy slowly and painfully died in the car three to four hours later.

The beating was witnessed by the grandmother and aunt. They did nothing to try and stop the beatings. After the man had beaten the boys and driven away, they did not call the police, nor Child Protective Services, nor other relatives, nor friends. They did not reach out to anyone to help these innocent children.

Had the grandmother or the aunt phoned SOMEONE, ANYONE, an individual they trusted, or law enforcement, the two-year-old boy might be alive today.

The story above is true. It happens every day throughout Texas and the United States. Child abuse does not limit itself to physical abuse, as described above. The abuse can also be neglectful, emotional, and/or sexual. The grandmother and aunt, acting as passive, uninvolved observers, did not honor a very basic principle – THE WILLINGNESS TO GET INVOLVED! It is so elementary and yet so vital!

Sgt. Bill Davis was the police detective in the story.

"A Willingness to Get Involved" was written by Sgt. Bill Davis. This story has been published in state and national publications.

Challenge – If we as adults don't help our children, our future, our greatest resource, my question to you is, **WHO WILL?**

And **why** should we get involved?
The answer for all of us is so simple...

**They are all somebody...because,
God doesn't make Junk!
and,
God doesn't make Mistakes!**

THOUGHTFUL POEMS

The Starfish Flinger

As the old man walked the beach at dawn,
he noticed a young man picking up starfish
and flinging them into the sea.
Catching up to the youth, he asked
him why he was doing this.
The answer was that the stranded starfish
would die if left in the morning sun.
"But the beach goes on for miles and there
are millions of starfish," countered the old
man.
"How can your effort make any difference?"
The young man looked at the starfish in his
hand and threw it to safety in the waves.
"It makes a difference to this one," he said,

Author Unknown

My question to <u>you</u> is, *"Will you make a positive difference to just one child? If you will, then I want you to make a positive difference to another one, and then one more."*
Sgt. Bill Davis

Tears of a Cop

I have been where you fear to be.
I have seen what you fear to see.
I have done what you fear to do.
All these things I have done for you.
I am the one you lean upon.
The one you cast your scorn upon.
The one you bring your troubles to.
All these people I've been for you.
The one you ask to stand apart.
The one you feel should have no heart.
The one you call the officer in blue.
But I am human, just like you.
And through the years I've come to see
That I am not what you ask of me.
So take this badge and take this gun.
Will you take it?
Will anyone?
And when you watch a person die,
And hear a battered baby cry,
Then so you think that you can be
All those things you ask of me?

        Author Unknown

Police Officer's Prayer

Lord, I ask for courage:
Courage to face and conquer my own fears…
Courage to take me where others will not go.

I ask for strength:
Strength of body to protect others.
Strength of spirit to lead others.

I ask for dedication:
Dedication to my job to do it well…
Dedication to my community to keep it safe.

Give me, Lord, concern:
For all those who trust me…
And compassion for those who need me.

And please, Lord,
Through it all, be at my side.
Amen

                                    Unknown

Sgt. Bill

He writes his books; He lived the story.
He talks for the victims in their pain and glory.
He helps all he can; It's sad but true.
He forms the line between the evil and the blue.
For many years, he has stood time's test.
He has made the grade. He is one of the best.
He is great for the kids, and he loves them as well.
He works tirelessly for them;
And gives his all you can tell.
When you read his books, you will know I am right.
His dedication is there. He fights the good fight.

By: Mr. Frosty Dryden
2017

"Taking Care of Children"

We're so proud of Sgt. Bill Davis,
and appreciate the talk he just gave us.
Taking Care of Children, he showed us the way.
Sgt. Bill Davis just saved the day.

He champions the cause of the abused child,
for he knows what they suffer is tragic, never mild.
If there is a hero in the making to be,
we submit his name for it should be he.

We are all now aware of the abused child's plight,
their struggle to survive and be alright.
We've heard their cries and the voices that plead,
and will endeavor to do whatever the need.

We know your work is never done.
We'll help you do your duty, and then some.
Tell us what you need and where?
We'll come running. We'll be there!

Author: Deborah F. Carter
St. Charles Women's Guild
November 5, 2002

SGT. BILL DAVIS

HISTORY

Sgt. Bill Davis
(409) 409-781-5726

Education:
1968   Graduated from Port Neches-Groves High School, Port Neches, TX
1968 – 1970 Attended East Texas Baptist University, Marshall, Texas
             Major: Business Administration   Minor: English
1971   Attended Lamar University, Beaumont, TX
             Major: Business Administration
             Total college hours – 106

Law Enforcement Career:
- August 20, 1971 to January 17, 1972
    Port Arthur, Texas Police Department, Patrol Officer
- September - October, 1971
    Attended the Lamar University Basic Police Academy
- June 06, 1972 to October 17, 1972
    Beaumont, Texas Police Department Patrol Officer
- February 17, 1973 to January 31, 2008
    Beaumont, Texas Police Department
- January 31, 2008
    Honorably Retired from the Beaumont, Texas Police Dept. with 35-years, 8-months, and 10-days of active law enforcement service
- February 1, 2008 to March 31, 2013
    State law enforcement commission carried by the Chambers County, Texas Sheriff's Department
- April 11, 2013 to May 23, 2018
    State law enforcement commission carried by the Kountze, Texas Police Department
- July 2018 to Present
    Texas law enforcement commission is carried by the Vidor, Texas Police Department

Currently holds the following certificates from the Texas Commission on Law Enforcement:
- Master Peace Officer's Certificate
- Instructor's Certificate
- Firearms Instructor's Certificate
- Traffic Safety Instructor's Certificate
    (developed and presented a program to seat belt violators)

Texas Commission on Law Enforcement training hours:
    4,068 In-Service Training Hours
(As a commissioned Texas Peace Officer, 40 hours of in-service training are required bi-annually.)

Assignments:
- June 6, 1972 to October 17, 1972 – Patrol Officer
- February 17, 1973 to October 9, 1977 – Patrol Officer, Patrol Division
- October 9, 1977 – Promoted to Sergeant

Assignments As Sergeant:
- Investigator in the Detective Division
- Child Abuse Investigator in the Special Crimes Bureau
- Investigator in the Crime Stoppers Unit
- Dispatcher in the Communications Division
- Supervising Sergeant in the Police Community Relations Unit
- Senior Investigating Sergeant in the Sex Crimes Unit of the Special Crimes Bureau
- B.P.D.'s Senior Supervising Sergeant and Interim Lieutenant of the Patrol Division – Day Shift for ten years

1976 – 1991
- Member of the Beaumont, Texas Police Department Special Weapons and Tactics Unit (S.W.A.T.).
- Main assignment – Sniper

1979 to Present
- Investigated over 7,000 child physical and sexual and adult sexual incidents

Accomplishments:
- Ongoing expertise: Child abuse and sexual abuse investigations, and adult sex crime investigations.

- Development and presentation of numerous public awareness programs, locally, throughout Texas, nationally, and internationally.

- July 28, 1983 to Present – Developed the following programs:
    Child Abuse: A National Epidemic
    Child Safety: First & Forever with Officer Bill
    Sex and the Law
    Personal Safety: A Fact of Life
    Bullies in Schools as it Relates to Domestic Violence for school staff development
    Legal Requirements to Report Pregnant Teens as a Victim of Child Abuse, and
    Sexual Predators: Identifying and Reporting

    These programs have been presented to over 315,000 people throughout Texas, the United States, and internationally.

- 1983 to 2012 – Bi-annual presenter at the Lamar Institute of Technology Regional Law Enforcement Academy for the Texas Commission on Law Enforcement's mandated Child Abuse Core Course. Currently, the most tenured guest speaker at the Academy.

- January 7, 1984 – Was accidently shot by a friend with a .12 gauge shotgun in the right hand, right forearm, and abdomen. Several operations and more than a year of extensive therapy now allow Bill to use this negative incident in a positive way, teaching gun safety to children during the *'Child Safety: First & Forever with Officer Bill'* program. It is the incident that instigated the writing of Bill's third book:

    LOOK OUT SATAN ~ GOD'S AT WORK!

- 1984 – Bill wrote the Beaumont Police Department's brochure, *'Facts on Child Abuse.'* 50,000+ copies of this brochure were distributed nationally.

- 1985 – Assigned to Beaumont Police Department's 'Crime Stoppers' unit.

- 1985 & 1991 – Received the *'Texas Congress of PTA's Honorary Life Membership Award'* from the Beaumont Metropolitan Area Council of PTAs for volunteer work with children.

- June 1, 1987 – One of two sergeants assigned to develop and supervise the Beaumont Police Department's new 'Police-Community Relations Unit.'

- 1987 – Wrote an article, *'The Willingness to Get Involved.'* It has been printed in several state and national publications and brochures.

- October, 1987 to September, 1991 – Developed a program for seat belt violators that was presented to 20,000+ people and greatly assisted in causing a significant reduction in the number of traffic fatality and injury accidents in Beaumont, as well as a reduction in the total number of accidents during those years.

- September 5, 1991 – Received the *'Governor's Award in the Field of Law Enforcement'* for crime victim's assistance at the Texas Crime Victim's Clearinghouse Conference.

- 1984 to 1991 – Appointed Chairman to the Beaumont City Council's Advisory Commission for the Prevention of Child Abuse and Neglect.

- 1985 to 1990 – Member of the Board of Directors for the state organization, Prevent Child Abuse Texas, in Austin, Texas.

- 1990 to 2012 – Founding Member and Longest Serving Member of the Board of Directors of the Garth House – The Mickey Mehaffy Children's Advocacy Center in Beaumont.

- January 4, 1994 – Received the *'First Annual Southwestern Bell Operators Community Involvement Award'* for work done with and for child physical and sex crime victims and adult sex crime victims above and beyond the call of duty.

- April 1994 – One of the top five finalists for the Beaumont Police Department's 1993 *'Officer of the Year'* award.

- June 12, 1994 – Received the *'Star Award'* from the Texas Corrections Association at their annual conference in Irving, Texas.

- August 24, 1994 – Received the *Master Peace Officer* certification from the Texas Commission on Law Enforcement.

- February 9, 1995 – Two local attorneys contributed $50,000 to the Garth House in Bill's honor for his work on a child molestation investigation that led to a life sentence for the perpetrator and a multi-million dollar lawsuit settlement for the eight-year-old victim. August 31, 1995, the Garth House Board of Directors used these funds to create a foundation to help support the Garth House.

- April 18, 1996 – The children's safety program, *'Child Safety: First & Forever with Officer Bill'* became available on video tape and CD, sponsored by Community Banks. The program is also available in coloring book form for children.

- November 7, 1996 – Received the *'1996 Texas Exemplary Layperson of the Year Service Award'* from the Texas Counseling Association at their state conference in Fort Worth, Texas.

- December 12, 1998 – Bill's first true crime book, <u>So Innocent, Yet So Dead</u>, was published. A second printing was published August, 2003 after the defendant's execution. 50,000+ copies have been sold. The book is available in print or as an e-book through Amazon.com.

- May, July, & September, 1999 – Presented child abuse seminars as a member of a three-person team for the U.S. Department of Justice and the U.S. Agency for International Development (U.S.A.I.D.), conducting educational seminars on the investigation and prosecution of child physical and sexual abuse crimes in El Salvador.

- February 22, 2001 – Received the *'Kinder Award for Art and Literature'* from Memorial Hermann Hospital, Houston, Texas and Houston's University of Texas Medical Branch-Kinder Clinic, a clinic which treats alcohol and drug dependent born children, for Bill's child abuse programs and his true crime novel.

- 1991 to Retirement, January 31, 2008 – Beaumont Police Department's most decorated officer.

- September 13, 2012 – A local attorney contributed $10,000 to the Women's and Children's Shelter of Southeast Texas in Bill's honor.

- April 1, 2016 – Bill's second true crime book, *Imperfect Love ~ Imperfect Justice*, was published. This book is available in print or as an e-book through Amazon.

- April, 2023 - Bill's third book, *Look Out Satan ~ God's At Work!*, an inspirational Christian book, was published.

Religion: A Christian!

Personal Achievements:
- A Texas Peace Officer for 50-years, and still counting!
- A Master Mason since January 14, 1974.

Family: Bill and Cheryl married in 2018. Their family includes three sons, three daughters-in-law, surrogate daughter and family. Together they share twelve grandchildren: nine girls and three boys.

Hobbies: Bill enjoys playing golf, weightlifting, and trying to stay in shape. He also enjoys hunting, fishing, camping, traveling with Cheryl, and spending time with relatives and friends.

TRUE CRIME BOOKS BY SGT. BILL DAVIS

Bill Davis's First True Crime Book

So Innocent, Yet So Dead
ISBN: 978-0-9850403-8-3

On October 6, 1990, during a family weekend at a local trade show in Beaumont, Texas, Joe and Elaine Langley's life changed forever. Their ten-year-old daughter, Falyssa Van Winkle, disappeared while buying a bag of peanuts just a few yards away. She should have never been found. Five hours after her disappearance, her body was found under a rural bridge, sixty-miles from Beaumont. She had been raped and killed. Starting with hundreds of potential witnesses and suspects who were at the trade show that day, a team of law enforcement investigators from throughout Southeast Texas quickly narrowed their focus to a forty-four year old vendor and family acquaintance named James Rexford Powell. Seen through the eyes of a veteran sex crimes detective who helped lead the search for Falyssa Van Winkle's killer, this book is a chronicle of the investigation, arrest, and subsequent trial of a man whose profile is all too familiar to law enforcement.

Sgt. Davis obtained the trial transcript. Testimony is quoted in the book just as it appears in the trial transcript. He makes you feel as if you are one of the jurors. Powell was convicted of capital murder by the jury in forty-five minutes. He was sentenced to death by the jury in thirty-five minutes. This is one of the fastest, if not **THE** fastest, that anyone has been convicted of capital murder and sentenced to death anywhere in the United States since the U.S. Supreme Court re-established the death penalty in 1976.

James Rexford Powell was executed for his crimes on October 1, 2002. Joe and Elaine Langley did not want to attend the execution, but asked the Texas Department of Justice to allow Sheriff Powell and Sgt. Bill Davis to attend on their behalf. It's rare, but the request was granted. After witnessing Rex Powell take his last breath, and after much research, an additional chapter was added to the book covering issues that occurred during Powell's eleven years and nine months on death row. Readers have remarked that Bill is so illustrative in his description of October 1, 2002 events at the execution, they felt as though they were standing beside Bill, watching Powell take his last breath.

The information and facts in this book will help you protect your children and grandchildren against predators like James Rexford Powell who are walking amongst us.

SO INNOCENT, YET SO DEAD

The true story of the kidnapping, rape and murder of a 10-year-old child, and the investigation and trial that followed.

2nd Printing Final Chapter

Written by
BILL DAVIS
A Police Detective Who Investigated the Crime.

Bill Davis's Second True Crime Book

Imperfect Love ~ Imperfect Justice
ISBN: 978-0-9850403-7-6

Martha entered her home and put the groceries in the foyer. Her need to use the bathroom was urgent. "Next!" she called out, as was the custom in their home. Her husband suddenly appeared through the make-shift curtain covering the entrance to the second-floor bathroom of their home, and descended the stairs wearing only his boxer shorts. As she ascended the stairs, she heard the quiet voice of her eleven-year-old daughter, "I'm almost dressed. I'm hurrying."

Martha's world suddenly turned upside down. She had two children to protect. Where would she go? What should she do? What would she do?

Travel with Sgt. Davis as he takes you through the extensive investigation that covers several Southeast Texas counties, as well as a mountaintop ranch in far West Texas. Sit with the jurors as they hear candid testimony of how a master manipulator managed to sexually molest his own daughter for over seven years.

Quotes from Tori's interview and affidavit with Sgt. Davis are in the book. Sgt. Davis acquired the transcript from this trial. As the last chapter covering the trial is read, the quotations from the trial's transcript make you feel as if you are a juror listening to the testimony.

PRESENTATIONS BY SGT. BILL DAVIS

Child Abuse: A National Epidemic

Sgt. Bill Davis takes you on a roller-coaster ride, laughing one minute and crying the next with his inspired presentation about crimes against the most precious and innocent element of society - **our children**. Using almost 500 slides, he educates his audience about physical, neglect, emotional, and sexual abuses to children and how child abuse and domestic violence intermingle. He will discuss applicable laws, physical abuse indicators, wound identification, shaken baby syndrome, S.I.D.S., profiles of the three kinds of rapists, profiles of the three kinds of pedophiles, incestuous families, positive parenting skills, and ways to curtail and report these incidents of abuse and violence. The program is adapted as a 45-minute program, a 4-hour lecture, or an 8-hour seminar. It's a program you can't say you enjoyed, but it's one **you will never forget**. The information you receive just **might save a child's life**.

Child Safety: First & Forever with Officer Bill

When it's time to teach safety to children, Sgt. Bill Davis becomes 'Officer Bill' to his 'little friends.' Officer Bill's child safety program is presented to elementary school students in three time frames: 22-minutes for pre-k and kindergarten, 33-minutes for 1st and 2nd graders, and 45-minutes for 3rd, 4th, and 5th graders. Officer Bill begins by introducing our 'heroes,' our military and first responders to students. He then discusses gun safety, bicycle safety, and seat belt safety. He reinforces their right to say "NO" to drugs and crime. Officer Bill also discusses 'bullying' in all three presentations. Lastly, he deals with the sensitive issues of 'good touches,' 'bad touches,' and the 'UH-OH touches' (with grades 1st - 5th) in a very sensitive, understanding, and positive manner. Officer Bill's interaction with children keeps their attention at a constant high level.

Personal Safety: A Fact of Life

Many times in modern society, our work and/or our daily routine takes us out of the safety and security of our homes, offices, and other places of employment and into places and situations that can put our safety at great risk. Some professions require home visits or interviews on a violator's turf. We cannot help children, or others, if we are injured, raped, or killed. Sgt. Davis presents some common-sense ideas and a few defensive tactics to help us maintain a higher level of awareness and safety at home, our workplace, and in our vehicles as we work, travel, or go through our daily routine. The ideas presented in this program just might save your life.

Bullies in Schools in Relationship to Domestic Violence

One of the greatest problems facing schools today is the issue of bullying. School districts are being held criminally and civilly liable every day because they did too much, or too little concerning bullies and school violence issues. Sgt. Davis discusses issues from a U.S. Dept. of Justice study and a 2017 Texas Law, *'David's Law,'* defining bullying issues and new criminal liabilities. He intertwines school issues with domestic violence and sexual issues. Sgt. Davis discusses where bullying starts, he defines bullying and how the definition intermingles with the law, and why so many bullying victims are reluctant to report bullying incidents. He will discuss how a 'zero tolerance' policy is counter-productive and how school districts are being sued in federal court for not addressing their bullying problems. Sgt. Davis's program will show parents how they can be held accountable civilly for not stopping their child from being a bully at school.

Legal Requirements to Report Pregnant Teens as a Victim of Child Abuse

Thought: If someone tried to steal your purse and in the scuffle, knocked you down and broke your arm (the incident is no longer a theft, it's a robbery), would you call the police?

Thought: If an intoxicated driver crashed into a vehicle occupied by your child or grandchildren and killed them (vehicular manslaughter), would you call the police?

Thought: If a child you knew who was 16-years-old or younger and became pregnant, would you call the police?

All of the incidents listed above, including having sex with a child, someone 16-years-of-age or younger, are 2nd degree felony crimes, under Texas law, punishable by the possibility of 2 to 20 years in prison. And, having sex with a child 13-years-of-age or younger is a 1st degree felony, punishable by the possibility of 5 to 99 years or life in prison (the same punishment received for the crime of murder). Sgt. Davis, a veteran child abuse and sex crimes detective, presents his 60 - 90 minute program using Texas criminal and civil laws to show our responsibilities and liabilities in dealing with pregnant teenagers. He will explain how a police investigation MUST occur with every pregnant teen, 16-years old or younger.

Sexual Abuse: Identifying and Reporting

Sgt. Davis has investigated more than 7,000 child abuse and sex crime cases. In this presentation, he discusses the elements of some of the most often used criminal statutes dealing with child abuse and sex crime incidents. He discusses the profiles of the three types of rapists, the three types of pedophiles, and how these predators are able to get away with years of victimization. Sgt. Davis also discusses the Texas mandatory child abuse reporting statute and how to properly use this statute for the child and the person reporting the allegation.

Sex and the Law

Most adults are reluctant to talk to teenagers about SEX. Sgt. Davis's 90-minute program IS NOT a sex education program. Very candidly and professionally, he discusses the various criminal laws dealing with the sexual encounters that relate to anyone 10-years-of-age or older. Sgt. Davis also addresses civil laws dealing with pregnancy, paternity suits, child support, and the rights of the mother, father, and child. The program is filled with audience participation, laughter, anxiousness, and undivided attention from his audience. This program is Sgt. Davis's most requested program. It has helped thousands of teenagers make right decisions for their life instead of wrong decisions that could negatively affect them for the rest of their life.

The front page of Bill's tri-fold brochure every teenager receives after attending his 'Sex and the Law' Program.

Sex and the Law

by Sgt. Bill Davis
Beaumont, Texas

Sgt. Davis has always told young people they are accountable for their actions. Young people should be made aware of the laws they are held accountable to in their daily lives. As a veteran police officer since 1971, Sgt. Davis has investigated over 7,000 child abuse and sex crime incidences. Sgt. Davis travels throughout Texas and the United States talking to adolescents and teenagers about safety issues and laws applicable to their daily lives. One of the major issues facing young people today are issues dealing with sex. His 90-minute program for teenagers very professionally and candidly discusses criminal and civil laws dealing with this sensitive issue. This brochure covers some of the highlights of his program.

PHOTOS

Who is this?

More than 40 years ago, this wide-eyed wonder kid had his sights firmly set on something beyond the camera lens — a trait that is today the hallmark of his life's work: the vision to know there is often more to a situation than meets the eye, and his ability to help people in those situations. See answer on page 38.

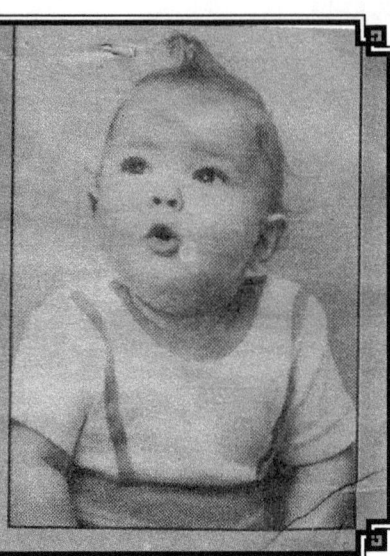

THE EXAMINER - Aug. 13 - 19, 1998

Answer: Who is this?

(from page 30)

Sgt. Bill Davis of the Beaumont Police Department's Special Crimes Bureau, Sex Crimes Unit works with and for abused children. His determination to see that offenders are brought to justice has earned him boundless respect and countless thanks from the community.

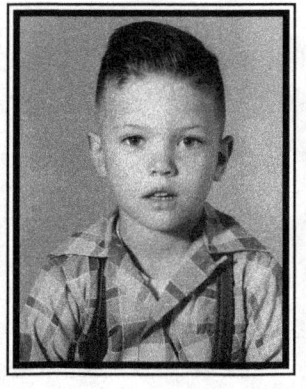

Growing up in Groves, Texas

Sgt. Bill Davis

Detective/Sgt. Bill Davis

Even in retirement, Sgt. Davis continues to be a Licensed Texas Peace Officer.

3 Generations of the Davis Family

**Bill
Dusty
Kaelyn**

Ashley Merritt Photography

Bill and his Granddaughter Kaelyn

Safest
Little Girl
In The World

Bill loves to give Cheryl pretty flowers.

On a whim, Bill stopped beside the roadside and picked some buttercup flowers for Cheryl.

**Bill and Cheryl on their wedding night,
November 17, 2018**

A Blessing

May the Lord bless you and keep you.

May the Lord make His face to shine upon you,

And be gracious to you.

May He give you peace.

May you receive a fresh touch of

Supernatural blessing from Heaven above.

You are divinely destined to accomplish the purpose

God has for you, and nothing on this earth can stop you.

Heaven has anointed you to fulfill God's destiny through you.

Walk in peace and grace in the best of times.

God is holding you in the palm of his hand.

In the worst of times,

He has you right in the same place,

Where no one can touch you.

He will make you the head and not the tail,

And all that you put your hand to shall prosper.

In Jesus name, Amen.

www.ingramcontent.com/pod-product-compliance
Lightning Source LLC
Chambersburg PA
CBHW071432150426
43191CB00008B/1101